SpringerBriefs in Business

SpringerBriefs present concise summaries of cutting-edge research and practical applications across a wide spectrum of fields. Featuring compact volumes of 50 to 125 pages, the series covers a range of content from professional to academic. Typical topics might include:

- A timely report of state-of-the art analytical techniques
- A bridge between new research results, as published in journal articles, and a contextual literature review
- A snapshot of a hot or emerging topic
- An in-depth case study or clinical example
- A presentation of core concepts that students must understand in order to make independent contributions

SpringerBriefs in Business showcase emerging theory, empirical research, and practical application in management, finance, entrepreneurship, marketing, operations research, and related fields, from a global author community.

Briefs are characterized by fast, global electronic dissemination, standard publishing contracts, standardized manuscript preparation and formatting guidelines, and expedited production schedules.

More information about this series at http://www.springer.com/series/8860

Philipp von Carlowitz

Success in the Bottom of the Pyramid Market in Africa

The Case of Multinational Pharmaceutical Companies

Springer

Philipp von Carlowitz
ESB Business School
Reutlingen University
Reutlingen, Germany

ISSN 2191-5482 ISSN 2191-5490 (electronic)
SpringerBriefs in Business
ISBN 978-3-030-59067-3 ISBN 978-3-030-59068-0 (eBook)
https://doi.org/10.1007/978-3-030-59068-0

This Springer imprint is published by the registered company Springer Nature Switzerland AG.
The registered company address is: Gewerbestrasse 11, 6330 Cham, Switzerland

Preface

Thinking about Africa the perspective is often that of poverty. At the same time, an increasing interest in collaboration between development cooperation agencies and private companies to strengthen the business activities on the African continent can be observed. In this context, the question that constantly arises is how to directly combine business activities with poverty alleviation. The belief that a lasting contribution of private business to reducing poverty and raising living standards is only possible with a profitable setup led to the question as to how business can create a profitable business model with the poorer population segments, the bottom of the pyramid (BoP). In order to make it relevant for business, the idea of an applied research publication arose: Based on literature findings, practical success factors are derived and a framework is developed that can be a guidance for companies interested in addressing the bottom of the pyramid in Africa.

After some initial research, it became apparent that a for-profit logic in the context of the bottom of the pyramid is not a very dominant perspective in research. Rather, the focus lies on social and inclusive business models where profitability is of secondary importance. Also, little focus was given to BoP business models in Sub-Saharan Africa, as most literature and case studies focus on the South Asian region. These two findings led to the idea for this book. The decision to choose the pharmaceutical industry was a result of the relevance of health in the Sustainability Development Goals and its high relevance for living standards of the poor population. Also, some multinational pharmaceutical companies are already attempting to address the bottom of the pyramid in Sub-Saharan Africa, which made it feasible to add an empirical part to the analysis via expert interviews, thus enhancing the practical approach of this book.

I want to thank Hannah Zedler, who conducted the interviews. Thanks also go to the experts from the multinational pharmaceutical companies that made time for the expert interviews, adding practical insights to the analysis. Further thanks go to the team at Springer Publishers, namely Rocio Torregrosa and Daniel Jagadisan. For his excellent proofreading I am grateful to Mike Seymour. Lastly I would like to thank my family, who supported me during my work on this book.

Contents

About the Author

Philipp von Carlowitz teaches and researches at the ESB Business School of Reutlingen University. Previously, he worked in various strategy functions at BASF SE and Siemens AG. His research in strategic and international management is applied, seeking theoretically and conceptually based practical insights that can help companies and institutions to be successful. His main field of research is business in Sub-Saharan Africa. He has published in this field on topics such as distribution challenges in Africa, entrepreneurship in Africa, and doing business in Africa. He has conducted studies on business in Africa that were published for various government institutions such as the German Federal Ministry for Economic Cooperation and Development, Austrian Federal Minister for Digital and Economic Affairs, Austrian Development Agency, and the Austrian Economic Chambers (WKO). He is also an advisor on Africa and general strategic management topics to private companies, for example, Siemens AG, BASF SE, and B. Braun Melsungen AG. He is a member of the scientific advisory board of the German-African Business Association (Afrika-Verein der deutschen Wirtschaft) and the International Trade Committee of the Chamber of Commerce Reutlingen.

List of Abbreviations

AfDB	African Development Bank
AHS	African Health Strategy
bn	billion
BoP	Bottom of the pyramid
CAGR	Compound annual growth rate
e.g.	exempli gratia ('for example')
et al.	et alia ('and others')
FDI	Foreign direct investment
fob	free on board
GDP	Gross domestic product
giz	Gesellschaft für international Zusammenarbeit
i.e.	id est ('that is to say')
ICT	Information and communication technology
IMF	International Monetary Fund
IFPMA	International Federation of Pharmaceutical Manufacturers & Associations
KPI	Key performance indicator
m	million
MNC	Multinational corporation
n.d.	no date
p.a.	per annum
PMPA	Pharmaceutical Manufacturing Plan for Africa
PPP	Purchasing power parity
SSA	Sub-Saharan Africa
UN	United Nations
UNCTAD	United Nations Conference on Trade and Development
UNDP	United Nations Development Programme
UNECA	United Nations Economic Commission for Africa
UNESCO	United Nations Educational, Scientific and Cultural Organization
USD	United States Dollar
VA	Value-Added

WEF	World Economic Forum
WHO	World Health Organization
WTO	World Trade Organization

List of Figures

List of Tables

Chapter 1
Introduction

Sub-Saharan Africa (SSA) is one of the most dynamic regions in the world. This is why companies worldwide have increasingly stepped up their activities on the continent. At the same time, however, Africa is the continent with the highest share of poor people worldwide. Global poverty remains a major issue with 10% of the world's population living on less than USD1.90 (PPP) and 26% living on less than USD3.20 (PPP) per day in 2015. In Sub-Saharan Africa, the shares are even higher, with 41% (421 m people) and 67% (678 m people), respectively, in 2017 (World Bank n.d.). This poverty situation has two effects: First, the world community has agreed on the so-called *Sustainability Development Goals (SDGs) 2030* which aim to alleviate poverty and improve the lives of the poor (UN 2015). Goal 3 of the SDGs (ensure healthy lives and promote well-being for all at all ages) focuses on healthcare as a key component of a better life. This of course includes the availability of medicines for the poor. Second, the high absolute poverty numbers lead to a rising interest in the market segment of the poor population, the so-called Bottom of the Pyramid (BoP) (defined in Sect. 2.1). Multinational companies in particular see it as a new and untapped market (Hammond and Kramer 2007).

Addressing the Bottom of the Pyramid market is relevant to both the population and companies: The BoP population obtains access to products that are otherwise not accessible, helping them to improve their living conditions. For companies, the BoP segment is a large market in terms of people that is widely untapped due to the obstacles associated with the difficult business conditions. Various authors agree that, in order to profitably tap the Bottom of the Pyramid market, a new and specific business model is required, since the business environment and the customer profile is too different compared to the Top of the Pyramid market segment (see London 2008; London and Hart 2004; Pitta et al. 2008; Prahalad and Hammond 2004; Seelos and Mair 2007; Subrahmanyan and Gomez-Arias 2008). This is why Hart (2017), despite the interest and attractiveness by population size, argues:

P. von Carlowitz, *Success in the Bottom of the Pyramid Market in Africa*,
SpringerBriefs in Business, https://doi.org/10.1007/978-3-030-59068-0_1

> …most BoP ventures and corporate initiatives over the past decade have either failed outright or achieved only moderate success at great cost. (Hart 2017)

Simanis and Duke (2014) agree with this assessment:

> During the past decade, many multinationals have come up short trying to make a profit by solving the pressing needs of low-income communities.

They, however, continue to state:

> Profitably selling to the Bottom of the Pyramid is difficult, but can be done. (Simanis and Duke 2014).

It is only in more recent literature, starting with Prahalad and Hart (1999) and Prahalad and Hart (2002), that the concept of the Bottom of the Pyramid was introduced. Kolk et al. (2014) note that many cases and examples used originate from India and other emerging economies. A recent literature review by Dembek et al. (2019) reveals the still-nascent state of research on the Bottom of the Pyramid, especially with respect to Sub-Saharan Africa. Only a total of 279 peer-reviewed papers (between 2002 and 2016) focused on the BoP, of which only 49 papers (18% of total papers reviewed) dealt with the question of how multinational companies (MNCs) can be successful in the BoP. Only 22 papers are empirical studies and 29 publications focus exclusively on Africa. Hence, in order to broaden the empirical base, further research on the Bottom of the Pyramid in Africa is necessary.

This book will contribute to a number of gaps in the literature: It focuses on MNCs, it deals with Africa, and it includes an empirical section. The book's research question is:

> How can multinational pharmaceutical companies set up a profit generating business model when addressing the BoP in Sub-Saharan Africa?

The investigation focuses on the case of multinational pharmaceutical companies for three reasons: (1) Healthcare provision is one of the SDGs and thus of political relevance; (2) some multinational pharmaceutical companies are already engaging in activities to address the BoP market segment in Sub-Saharan Africa; and (3) pharmaceuticals are products that allow for a variety of distribution approaches.

The challenge when writing about the Bottom of the Pyramid is the mix of business issues on the one hand, and social impact and poverty alleviation on the other. Usually, terms that come to mind when discussing the BoP are social responsibility, aid, and inclusive business models. The focus is always on the social/poverty side. However, Sinkovics et al. (2014) found that there does not need to be an explicit "social" motive in a business venture targeting the BoP in order to generate social impact: Addressing the BoP with a profit motive usually results in some positive social effect. Thus, company profit and social benefit for the BoP population are not contradictory. This book focuses on the pure business side, trying to understand how a company can make a sustainable profit when addressing the BoP.

The structure of this book is as follows: The first two chapters explain the concept of the Bottom of the Pyramid concept in literature. Then the concept is combined with the theoretical approach of business models. The question of business model development in the BoP context is extensively discussed. Chapters 4 and 5 then set the stage for the analysis of the pharmaceutical companies' approach in Sub-Saharan Africa: First, the overall situation and especially operational business conditions are discussed. Second, the healthcare system and the pharmaceutical market conditions are investigated. In Chap. 6, the results of all previous chapters are empirically investigated and analyzed. The final chapter develops a conceptual framework as a result of the literature analysis and the empirical study results. It provides some recommendations to companies planning to engage at the Bottom of the Pyramid in Sub-Saharan Africa.

References

Dembek K, Sivasubramaniam N, Chmielewski DA (2019) A systematic review of the bottom/base of the pyramid literature: cumulative evidence and future directions. J Bus Ethics 1:1–18

Hammond AL, Kramer W (2007) The next 4 Billion: market size and business strategy at the base of the pyramid. World Resources Institute, Washington, DC

Hart SL (2017) BoP 2.0: The next generation of strategy for the base of the pyramid. Corp Stewardship:190–204

Kolk A, Rivera-Santos M, Rufín C (2014) Reviewing a decade of research on the "base/bottom of the pyramid" (BOP) concept. Bus Soc 53:338–377

London T (2008) The base of the pyramid perspective: a new approach to poverty alleviation. Acad Manag Proc 1:1–6

London T, Hart SL (2004) Reinventing strategies for emerging markets: beyond the transnational model. J Int Bus Stud 35:350–370

Pitta DA, Guesalaga R, Marshall P (2008) The quest for the fortune at the bottom of the pyramid: potential and challenges. J Consum Mark 25:393–401

Prahalad CK, Hammond AL (2004) Selling to the poor. Foreign Policy 142:30–37

Prahalad CK, Hart SL (1999) Strategies for the bottom of the pyramid: creating sustainable development. Ann Arbor. https://www.researchgate.net/profile/Stuart_Hart4/publication/268425222_Strategies_for_the_Bottom_of_the_Pyramid_Creating_Sustainable_Development/links/555b2b3508aeaaff3bfc0f66/Strategies-for-the-Bottom-of-the-Pyramid-Creating-Sustainable-Development.pdf. Accessed 18 Aug 2019

Prahalad CK, Hart SL (2002) The fortune at the bottom of the pyramid. Strat Bus 26:2–14

Seelos C, Mair J (2007) Profitable business models and market creation in the context of deep poverty: a strategic view. Acad Manag Perspect 21:49–63

Simanis E, Duke D (2014) Profits at the bottom of the pyramid. Harv Bus Rev 92:86–93

Sinkovics N, Sinkovics RR, Yamin M (2014) The role of social value creation in business model formulation at the bottom of the pyramid – implications for MNEs? Int Bus Rev 23:692–707

Subrahmanyan S, Gomez-Arias T (2008) Integrated approach to understanding consumer behavior at bottom of pyramid. J Consum Mark 25:402–412

UN (2015) Transforming our world: the 2030 agenda for sustainable development. United Nations, New York

World Bank (n.d.) World Development Indicator Database. https://data.worldbank.org/products/wdi. Accessed 4 Aug 2018

Chapter 2
The Bottom of the Pyramid Concept

The Bottom of the Pyramid concept is not that old but has undergone some significant discussion and change in perspective over the past 15 years since Prahalad and Hart (1999, 2002) first introduced the concept. During that time the understanding of what constitutes the BoP and how companies and scholars perceive it has changed from a pure market/customer perspective to a partnering perspective and has eventually gone beyond pure business topics. This chapter will first define the Bottom of the Pyramid segment before discussing the development of the BoP concept in literature and providing a critical assessment of the state of the BoP discussion.

2.1 The Bottom of the Pyramid as a Population Segment

The Bottom of the Pyramid is a socioeconomic concept that constitutes the largest but poorest population segment in the world. It forms the symbolic "base" of the income pyramid that is below the emerging middle class and the wealthy class (see Fig. 2.1).

London and Hart (2010) define BoP as the "low-income socio-economic segment that is not well-integrated into the formal economy." If the BoP is defined along income lines the question as to the meaning of "low-income" arises. There is still no consensus about the proper way to define the BoP (Dolfsma et al. 2009). According to the World Bank, the BoP technically comprises individuals with an annual income below USD2000 (in PPP). However, leading articles in academic and practitioner discussion use a per capita income at below USD1500 or 2000 per annum (Agnihotri 2012; Collier 2007) or even less than USD2 per day (in 1993 PPP) as a definition (Banerjee and Duflo 2007). Later, the authors started to segment the BoP sector into different income levels (low income, subsistence, extreme poverty) (Rangan et al. 2011). For the purpose of this book, extreme poverty is excluded and the focus lies on the upper two BoP segments (see Fig. 2.1).

P. von Carlowitz, *Success in the Bottom of the Pyramid Market in Africa*, SpringerBriefs in Business, https://doi.org/10.1007/978-3-030-59068-0_2

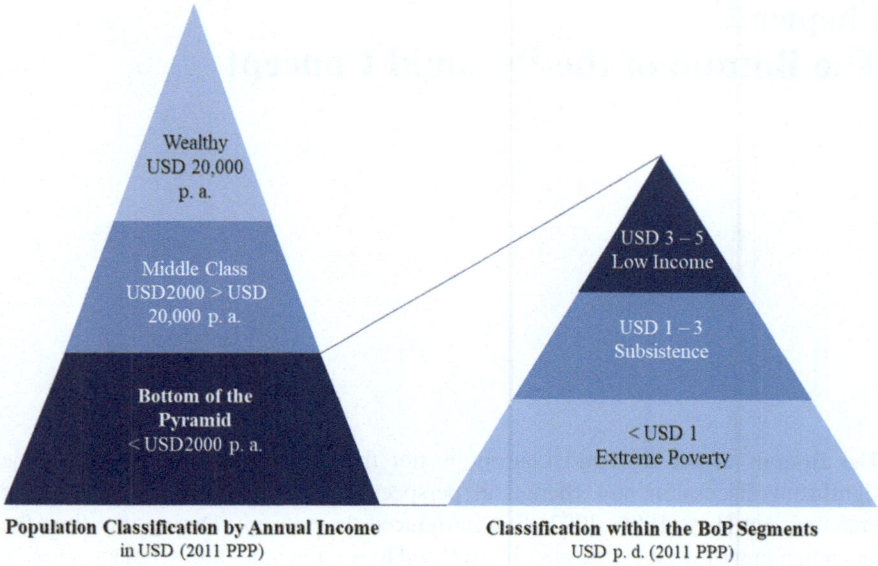

Fig. 2.1 World income pyramid and characteristics of the BoP population. Source: Own illustration, based on Banerjee and Duflo (2007) and Rangan et al. (2011)

The BoP is not to be confused with related terms such as "developing countries." Unlike the classification of states according to different criteria of economic and social development, the BoP is characterized as a cross-national segment of the population (Hahn 2009). Hence, people in industrialized countries can live in poverty and also belong to the BoP. What is known about the BoP is usually a composition of generalized statements. A common misconception is that the poor are a homogeneous group that will buy anything as long as it is cheap and available. In fact, characteristics vary enormously within and among countries and communities (Ahmed 2013). Besides the financial vulnerability, the *Human Development Report*, published by the United Nations Development Program (UNDP 2005), includes another three quantitative indices for a standard picture of "the poor": poor health status, gender inequity, and a high level of illiteracy. Narayan et al. (2000) add "marginalization" as a characteristic of "the poor" as a result of their qualitative field study. As Ahmed (2013) puts it:

> The culture of poverty is the culture of marginalization. The golden rule, silence, means survival. [. . .] They are reluctant to voice anger and disappointment to someone of a higher class. Poor customers also react differently to where and how a product is sold.

The BoP population is located in urban and rural areas. The urban poor population mostly lives in densely populated slum areas (Johnson 2007). In general, it has a higher per-capita income than the rural BoP population. Their purchasing power, however, is not necessarily higher, owing to above average living costs (Ireland 2008). The majority of people at the BoP live in scattered informal settlements in rural areas and are usually excluded from modern global societies (Prahalad and

Hammond 2002). The urban BoP is considered to be a more accessible market for companies as it is less dispersed than the rural BoP. The differentiation between rural versus urban BoP population is characterized by a greater distance to economic centers, wider dispersion, higher poverty levels, more widespread illiteracy, and even greater heterogeneity (Ireland 2008).

Management literature saw little potential for business engagement with the poor for a long time due to this challenging environment and the limited economic resources of the poor (Kolk et al. 2014). However, initial estimates of the size of this population segment put it at 4–5 billion people, that is nearly two-thirds of the world's population, spending an estimated USD5 trillion per annum (Mohr et al. 2012; Prahalad 2005). These figures make the BoP as a group an interesting target customer segment. However, for companies, it is difficult to address the BoP due to its fragmentation, low per capita purchasing power, and challenging logistical access. Prahalad and co-authors like Hart and Hammond attracted considerable attention when they claimed that there was a profit to be made in BoP markets despite difficult business conditions. In their articles, the authors propose possible courses of action for companies to succeed in these underserved markets while simultaneously helping to alleviate poverty (Hahn 2009).

2.2 Characterizing the Bottom of the Pyramid Market and Consumers

Researchers agree that the BoP market exhibits entirely different characteristics to high-income markets (Galariotis et al. 2011; Gold et al. 2013; Hart and Christensen 2002). Tarafdar et al. (2011) emphasize the significant limitation of consumption and choice of goods because of the dependence on informal markets, which usually have lower quality and higher prices, as the major problems for the poor. Also, the effort they must make in order to obtain goods and services in comparison to higher income groups is greater (Hammond and Kramer 2007). Consumers at the BoP are uniquely dependent on local distributors or other intermediaries who are likely to exploit them by controlling prices (Klein 2008; Sachs et al. 2004; Whitehead et al. 2001). Thus, various obstacles impede the efforts of the people at the BoP to improve their standard of living (Banerjee and Duflo 2007). In literature, authors refer to this as the "poverty trap" (Karnani 2005; Prahalad 2005).

In their book, Prahalad and Hammond (2002) describe the consequences of the poverty trap as being significant unmet needs of the poor. They have no means to meet basic needs, no access to modern financial services, and no access to formal competitive markets (Prahalad 2005; Prahalad and Hammond 2002; Schuster and Holtbrügge 2012). Contrary to popular opinion, the lack of essential goods such as food and clean water is no reason for multinational corporations to avoid the BoP market. Instead, Prahalad (2005) describes the unmet needs of the people at the BoP as an attractive business opportunity because of the size of this population segment (see Sect. 2.1). Although individuals own few economic resources each, it adds up to a USD5 trillion global consumer market that has remained more or less untapped so far (Hammond and Kramer 2007; Kuttalam 2012; Soto 2000). As others have pointed out, the BoP potentials discussed might be lower for most goods and services as poor consumers spend up to 80% of their income on necessities, leaving little disposable income for other offerings (Karnani 2007b). The result of all this is a "BoP dilemma" for managers: The total BoP market is of significant size but is spread across a large number of people and a fragmented population with low individual purchasing power. Hence, it is hard to address this market.

In the early literature, the perception was that there was one type of BoP consumer defined by a low income. Studies have recently challenged this perception. Authors have empirically argued that, while affordability is a defining variable for BoP consumers, additional variables such as the level of education, number of children, and age help to segment the BoP consumers further (Janda et al. 2018). In their study on South Africa's BoP Lappeman et al. (2019) find that a significant number of variables characterizing BoP consumers is country-specific in addition to the generic characteristics of BoP buyers. The general criteria for BoP consumers which they extract from literature are low income, vulnerability, high level of illiteracy, strong sense of community and partnership, (mobile) connectivity, concern about dignity and self-esteem, significant brand consciousness, and low trust in large (multinational) companies. Other authors add that BoP consumers do not usually have a constant and predictable revenue stream, live in relative isolation that creates (sub-)cultures different from other consumer segments, and exhibit strong social bonds (Chikweche and Fletcher 2012; Kuo et al. 2016). These differentiated views on BoP consumers are supported by an early study by Subrahmanyan and Gomez-Arias (2008). They investigated BoP consumer behavior in the context of Maslow's pyramid of needs. The results showed that consumers in the BoP market purchase products beyond "survival and physiological needs" and are willing to pay relatively higher prices for some goods that increase their social standing (e.g., education) or that are higher quality products ("luxury"). In the latter case, they are willing to purchase smaller volumes, in smaller packaging, in order to have access to these products. Another study showed that the role of brands in buying decisions might not be very different between BoP consumers and customers from higher income segments (Nagy et al. 2019). The highest spending increase in BoP consumption was on information and communication technology, which is a "higher order need." Much BoP consumption is social capital based, meaning it relates to social standing and maintaining social ties. Using the 4-P framework that is well known in marketing the authors find that successfully sold products are adapted by simplifying usage and packaging size. The pricing can be higher than expected, especially for products beyond the survival level. The willingness to pay for premium quality and products or services with high social capital exists at the BoP. Affordability, however, remains an issue. In terms of sales outlets, BoP consumers buy from local markets or neighborhood stores that mostly have an informal character. Promotion channels are billboards and word-of-mouth since the usual channels, like TV, are not feasible due to their lack of availability

(Chikweche and Fletcher 2012; Subrahmanyan and Gomez-Arias 2008). The authors conclude that localization is helpful when addressing the BoP:

> [...]building bonds with community and higher order needs such as self-esteem and self-fulfillment lead to greater productivity and profit opportunities. (Subrahmanyan and Gomez-Arias 2008)

These different characteristics of BoP consumers as opposed to higher income consumers have an impact on the requirements for a strong value proposition in BoP markets (see Sect. 3.1). Addressing the BoP market is thus more complex than merely dealing with customers' low purchasing power. A significant amount of (local) knowledge and understanding is required to set up a successful business. This realization is reflected in the shift of perception on BoP in the academic discourse. Management literature refers to the different views as the "BoP concept" (Kolk et al. 2014).

2.3 Bottom of the Pyramid: Conceptual Developments

Since its initial articulation (Prahalad and Hammond 2002) interest in gaining new insights about business at the BoP has continued to grow. An increasing number of authors have contributed to the understanding of the BoP concept. After nearly two decades of research, authors make a distinction between the "BoP Version 1.0" and "BoP Version 2.0" which were more recently supplemented by a "BoP 3.0" to structure existing literature (Caneque and Hart 2015). This chapter describes the evolution of the understanding of the Bottom of the Pyramid concept and how it has changed over time.

2.3.1 Bottom of the Pyramid Version 1.0

Initially BoP researchers proposed the idea that the entire private sector, but multinational corporations (MNCs) in particular, can further multiply their profits by tapping into the underserved BoP markets (Olsen and Boxenbaum 2009). Enterprises can capture attractive business opportunities at the BoP in a way that, at the same, time helps to alleviate poverty. Prahalad (2006) underpins this declaration by refuting and correcting widely accepted assumptions about the poor. A low income does not eliminate market processes. Even poor households use money or labor to meet basic needs and collectively they may offer a profitable scale of market-serving opportunities (Gupta and Khilji 2013). Three common misconceptions about the BoP are shown in Table 2.1.

In contrast to these misconceptions, the nature of the BoP market segment is that it is open for new technologies, that consumption rates are high (little saving), that consumers value quality while, at the same time, remaining price-sensitive due to

Table 2.1 Misconceptions and the real nature of the BoP market

Misconception about the BoP	Nature of the BoP market	Author
People at the BoP are neither interested nor can afford latest technologies/products/services	People at the BoP accept advanced technology rapidly. This is evidenced by the fast spread of wireless devices	Prahalad (2006)
People at the BoP use their savings to meet basic needs	People at the BoP are more concerned about their current consumption rather than savings for their future. They tend to indulge in buying products from their disposable income	Prahalad and Hammond (2002)
People at the BoP are not brand-conscious	People at the BoP are brand- and value-conscious by necessity. They expect good quality at an affordable price	Nagy et al. (2019), Prahalad (2006), and Subrahmanyan and Gomez-Arias (2008)

Source: Own illustration

their low-income levels. Thus, the authors conclude that the BoP offers business opportunities for private companies despite the individual low level of income.

The BoP population is active in informal systems. Therefore, before businesses can address BoP markets they need to create a (formal) market at the BoP and develop commercial infrastructure and institutions (Prahalad 2005; Prahalad and Hammond 2004; Prahalad and Hart 2002). From the perspective of Prahalad and Hart (2002), four strategic elements are relevant: (1) Create buying power, (2) shape aspirations, (3) improve access, and (4) local solutions are necessary. The elements are required to develop the BoP market by nurturing local markets and cultures, leverage local solutions, and generate wealth at the BoP (Prahalad and Hart 2002). These elements mutually influence each other. As Dolan and Roll put it:

> [. . .] business constitutes and develops the BoP, making the unknown frontier of 'unusable' Africa into a viable market for global capital. (Dolan and Roll 2013)

They draw up four steps to achieve this market development: (1) Identifying problems faced by the BoP population, (2) creating legitimacy, e.g., by partnering with an NGO, (3) describing proposed beneficiaries in the BoP segment, that is creating a customer profile and focusing on the need/benefit to be created, and (4) developing the market, creating consumers out of people, which implies creating customer aspirations and desires. This is fully in line with the arguments of Calton et al. (2013) who—as proponents of BoP 2.0—see this as only being achievable in a networked approach that integrates the BoP (see below).

The core of BoP version 1.0 is that this population segment is a large customer base that allows for high volumes, low prices, but low business margins. The by-product is a contribution to reducing poverty levels. From a business perspective, this implies adjusting the business approach in order to better address this customer segment in a profitable manner. Authors have expanded this purely sales/market perspective to a more cooperative approach.

2.3.2 *Bottom of the Pyramid Version 2.0*

A fast evolution of the BoP concept from the original emphasis on doing business with the poor to a broader, more strategic, framework can be noticed (Collier 2007; Kolk et al. 2014). More and more authors questioned key assumptions of the BoP concept 1.0 and raised justified concerns about the viability of MNCs taking a lead role in poverty alleviation (Agnihotri 2012; Bendell and Kearins 2005; Jenkins 2005; Karnani 2005; London and Hart 2004; Rollert 2011). Above all, Karnani (2005) is regarded as the main critic of Prahalad's work, calling the BoP concept "at best a harmless illusion and potentially a dangerous illusion [. . .]." In his analysis, he refutes the assumptions in BoP version 1.0 where the population is only seen as customers. He instead proposes viewing the poor as producers and emphasizes buying from them rather than selling to them. Other scholars also demanded a revised and more thorough examination of "the idea that MNC might simultaneously drive profit and mitigate poverty" (Simanis 2013) since this has not become a reality in his point of view.

This criticism led to the development of the BoP concept that requires an embedded process of co-creation (Simanis et al. 2008). As it was put:

> [. . .] we must caution that creating a fortune with rather than at the base of the pyramid requires more than merely changing a turn of phrase. (Calton et al. 2013)

The BoP community is thus regarded as an equal business partner who can be involved in value generation along the entire value chain, either as producer, distributor, or service provider, that opens up new possibilities to redesign value generation (see Sect. 3.1) (London and Hart 2011). New innovative approaches on how to address the BoP markets can be found by engaging in deep dialog with the poor (Simanis et al. 2008). This may help to ensure a business model that is culturally appropriate and sustainable. Further, there is a call to collaborate not only with the local people but also with NGOs and organizations on site with experience in BoP markets (Prahalad 2012). All this broadens the range of roles that the BoP population can play for business while raising the number of stakeholders, adding to the complexity. In literature, this new, inclusive approach is referred to as BoP 2.0 (Byerlee et al. 2007; Gold et al. 2013; Simanis et al. 2008; Tata et al. 2013). Figure 2.2 compares the perspective shift from BoP 1.0 to 2.0.

Reviewing the work of BoP 2.0 scholars, three strategic elements are described that facilitate successful business in BoP markets. These are:

1. Integrating BoP customers and local entrepreneurs to co-create products or services: This is based on the commonly accepted assumption that companies are likely to lack resources, knowledge, and expertise in the BoP environment. Cultural factors, in particular, are easily overlooked without local expertise during the development process. It is necessary to involve the local community in order to enable the business model development of suitable solutions for those markets (Schuster and Holtbrügge 2014).

BoP 1.0	BoP 2.0	
Converting BoP into consumer	BoP as business partner	BoP communities must be regarded as business partners that can play an active role along the entire value chain and not just passive consumers.
Gain insights through deep listening	Gain insights in deep dialogue	Companies have to engage in a deep dialogue with BoP communities to identify local needs.
Reduce price points	Expand imagination	A collaborative approach catalyzes business imagination and ensures the business model is culturally appropriate and environmentally sustainable by using local capabilities and resources.
Redesign packaging, extend distribution	Marry cababilities, build shared commitment and mutual value	Each stage of the process, not simply the new business, creates value for all partners.
Arm's length relationships mediated by NGOs	Direct, personal relationships facilitated by NGOs	MNCs need to work in equal partnership with local delivery providers, social development players, entrepreneurs, government officials and customers to imagine, launch, and grow sustainable business.
Selling to the Poor	**Business Co-Venturing**	

Fig. 2.2 BoP 1.0 versus BoP 2.0: From selling to the poor to business co-venturing. Source: Own illustration, based on Simanis et al. (2008)

2. Cooperating with non-traditional stakeholders such as NGOs: Partner with stakeholders that have expertise in overcoming obstacles in the BoP context such as the lack of adequate infrastructure or the high rate of corruption (London and Hart 2004). Without cooperation, companies are not able to create suitable products while minimizing costs and risks (Schuster and Holtbrügge 2012).
3. Building local capacity by improving the market conditions of low-income markets: Invest in the external business environment, which includes educating the local population, building local infrastructure, and creating employment (London and Hart 2004).

However, the assumption that, for instance, SMEs at the BoP are suitable partners to cooperate with international companies has been contested (Kowalkowski et al. 2013). It was stated that BoP entrepreneurs and individuals focus on survival and not on business growth as such (Ausrød et al. 2017). Calton et al. (2013) point out that a deep understanding of the BoP market and a multi-faceted stakeholder network is key to dealing with these challenges and to building a successful business at the BoP. They strongly argue for an integrated and cooperative business model. Bendul et al. (2017) find that integrating BoP stakeholders in the distribution activities of the BoP market is the most promising field for inclusiveness.

To sum up, BoP 2.0 is more concerned with cooperation between business and the BoP population going beyond the pure customer perspective of BoP 1.0. It is about creating a market—from generating the product or service all the way to selling it—as opposed to just "exploiting" it. A focus lies on stronger embeddedness in the BoP in order to understand and co-create suitable approaches: BoP as a partner, not just as a customer. This is in line with the idea of "inclusive" business models (see for instance UNDP 2013).

2.3.3 *Bottom of the Pyramid Version 3.0*

More recently another shift in the thinking about BoP markets has occurred, which some authors call BoP 3.0. It adds the component of sustainability and shifts the focus more on the topic of (social and environmental) value creation and ethical behavior toward the poor (Dembek et al. 2019). It has also been dubbed the "Sharing Fortune with BoP" idea (Borchardt et al. 2019). This is a shift away from a pure business focus. The idea of inclusiveness is pushed further by emphasizing the capacity for innovation and entrepreneurship and the sharing of knowledge across all stakeholders. By adding goals such as sustainability and ethics, the number of stakeholders increases, leading to even more complex and sophisticated cross-sector partnership structures between businesses, governments, NGOs, and civil society in general (van der Merwe et al. 2017). This stream of research is very recent and shifts the focus of analysis to a multidimensional definition of poverty and how companies addressing the BoP can contribute to alleviating it (Dembek et al. 2019).

Very recently a new version 4.0 has been proposed. It focuses on multinational companies. The acknowledgment of multinational companies having modern, ample, and significant resources leads to the idea that these should be deployed to tap into the BoP. It is meant to enable BoP firms to contribute to the MNC's BoP business by being viable partners, providing their local skills and knowledge (Borchardt et al. 2019). It remains to be seen whether it will become a new stream of thinking on the BoP.

2.3.4 *Emerging Research Streams and Focus Topics*

Apart from the pivotal work (Hart 2007; Prahalad and Hammond 2004; Simanis et al. 2008) that has shaped the term BoP and influenced the development of the general idea, many different subtopics have emerged. Many researchers have worked independently in niche areas. Besides the conceptual work, three further interrelated domains broadly shape today's academic discussion about business at the BoP. They are: Business as a means to achieve (international) economic development, a focus on specific individual business activities, and data-based analysis of the BoP as a market. These domains supplement the conceptual literature on the BoP (see Table 2.2).

One area that has been developed further, mainly by London (2007a, b), investigates the BoP as a tool for economic development primarily to support poverty alleviation. Like many other sociologists and organizational theorists in this field, the

Table 2.2 Overview of main research streams

Main research streams	Leading publications
Conceptual work	Strategies for the Bottom of the Pyramid: Creating Sustainable Development. (Prahalad and Hart 1999)
	Serving the World's Poor, Profitably. (Prahalad and Al Hammond 2002)
	Fortune at the Bottom of the Pyramid. (Prahalad 2005)
	Capitalism at the Crossroads. (Hart 2007)
	Misfortune at the Bottom of the Pyramid. (Karnani 2005)
	The Great Leap: Driving Innovation from the BoP. (Hart and Christensen 2002)
	The Base of the Pyramid Protocol: Beyond "Basic Needs" Business Strategies. (Simanis et al. 2008)
BoP as means for economic development	Reinventing Strategies for Emerging Markets. (London and Hart 2004)
	Base-of-the-pyramid Perspective on Poverty Alleviation. (London 2007a)
	The role of social value creation in business model formulation at the bottom of the pyramid—Implications for MNEs? (Sinkovics et al. 2014)
	Redefining Corporate Social Responsibility. (Porter et al. 2007)
BoP business activities in practice	Meeting Urgent Needs with Patient Capital. (Novogratz 2007)
	Connecting the Rural Poor to the World: Grameen's Village Phone in Bangladesh. (London 2007a, b)
	Doing Well By Doing Good: "Fair & Lovely" Whitening Cream. (Karnani 2007a)
	Unilever in India—Rural Marketing Initiatives. (Nagarajan 2006)
	Business Basics at the Base of the Pyramid. (Akula 2008)
	Is the bottom of the pyramid really for you. (Karamchandani et al. 2011)
	Socially responsible distribution: Distribution strategies for reaching the bottom of the pyramid. (Vachani and Smith 2008)
BoP market research and data	The Next 4 Billion: Market Size and Business Strategy at the Base of the Pyramid. (Hammond et al. 2007)
	Africa: A continent of opportunity for pharma and patients. (Holt et al. 2015)

Source: Own illustration

author calls for more accountability and more market-based approaches to development (London et al. 2010; London and Hart 2004).

Another strand of BoP research has turned to practical business topics. Investigations on the adaptation of the BoP approach with regard to specific operational issues such as adequate financing (Novogratz 2007), new distribution models (Vachani and Smith 2008), or design of BoP initiatives (Karamchandani et al. 2011) have become increasingly popular. A noteworthy trend that is being captured here is social capital investment opportunities such as microfinancing. Other papers address the push for innovative products that meet the needs of those living at the BoP (Karamchandani et al. 2011).

Far fewer publications are dedicated to market research and quantification of the market(s). The most remarkable work that estimates the size and composition of various BoP markets is the previously quoted "The next 4 Billion" (Hammond and Kramer 2007).

2.4 Criticism of the Bottom of the Pyramid Concept

The size of the BoP market was initially estimated to be 4 billion people and up to USD5 trillion (in PPP the value is estimated to be USD13 trillion) (Prahalad 2006). This has been assessed to be an overestimation since the household consumption figures of USD2 per day were said to be too high. The market size drops to USD1.2 trillion with a BoP population of 2.7 billion when assuming USD1.25 consumption spending (Karnani 2005). Using World Bank data, it was shown that the initial 4 billion population estimate for the BoP that could profitably be addressed is too high since it includes people living on less than USD1 per day (extreme poverty). Ignoring these very poor—which is in line with the approach of this book (see Sect. 2.1)—the number of addressable BoP population is nearly halved (Jaiswal 2008). This discussion shows the problems still surrounding the concept of the BoP itself: The divergence of definitions appearing in the literature results in confusion about what the BoP actually is. Consequently, studies are focusing on very different target populations and settings. Kolk et al. (2014) emphasize that authors need to be clear regarding their definition since blurred usage is likely to result in generalizations that make results questionable. The lack of accuracy has, in turn, fueled criticism of BoP research, especially by Karnani (2007a), who claims that most BoP initiatives discussed do not target the BoP but rather the emerging middle class in developing countries.

Others (Bonsu and Polsa 2011; Simanis 2011) agree with Karnani's (2005) criticism of business models operating at the BoP as theoretically and conceptually ambiguous. Simanis (2013) argues that the BoP is not yet a functioning market. There is no real marketplace for most products launched at the BoP, and companies fail to create the market which requires different strategies than common go-to-market approaches. This can be interpreted as a criticism of the one-sided focus of BoP 1.0 approaches. Others (Kolk et al. 2014) call for a realistic impact assessment to answer whether private organizations can alleviate poverty by doing business or whether it is even possible to gain a profit. Some researchers are skeptical and rather see MNCs' business operations to be just a new way of exploitation that does little to eradicate poverty but potentially hurts small businesses (Landrum 2007; Rashid and Rahman 2009; Warnholz 2007). Research still has to provide evidence-based answers.

The initial authors saw the possibility of creating a profitable business model for the BoP while reducing poverty (Prahalad 2006). Later this was questioned based on higher costs to serve the poor, specific BoP consumption behavior, and difficult access. It was also pointed out that there is a lack of empirical evidence to prove the point of profitable business (Agnihotri 2012; Jaiswal 2008; Karnani 2005). There is ample room to investigate, in detail and empirically, the actual potential to generate a profit when doing business with the BoP. To this end, more case studies on BoP business models are called for in research. Tashman and Marano (2010) emphasize that authors should begin to empirically analyze beneficial strategies that can be obtained from case studies. On this matter, Landrum (2007) disapproves of the fact that studies tend to ignore business failures. He highlights the obligation to study real failures in order to investigate the shortcoming of approaches. Simanis (2013) points out that researchers get too caught up with stunning theories and theoretical concepts without considering the pressure on managers to meet (global) sales targets. Ramachandran et al. (2012) and Nakata (2012) add that only a few scholars have investigated organizational structures, functional routines, and management practices that enable companies to establish business activities in BoP markets.

Many questions remain unanswered despite the growing academic interest in BoP markets. After almost two decades of research, the literature is only just beginning to understand the trade-offs that may exist between profitability, social impact, and the impact on the environment (Kolk et al. 2014). A better understanding of these interactions seems to be a crucial task for future research. Along this line, Schuster and Holtbrügge (2014) draw attention to the lack of empirical studies that apply sound theoretical frameworks. This is a regularly identified and major research gap.

Existing BoP literature predominantly consists of conceptual observation-based research, whereas only a few publications are based on large-sample data. Findings are often derived from a few case studies that cannot be applied universally (Kolk et al. 2014). By analyzing successful case studies, scholars focused on finding solutions related to buying (Omar et al. 2011), distributing (Vachani and Smith 2008), and marketing (Sheth 2011; van der Klein et al. 2012) at the BoP. There is a shortage of systematic and comprehensive studies of what a business model should look like as opposed to individual business activities.

2.5 Conclusion

Academic discussions with regard to BoP are ongoing and roughly 20 years old. The circumstances in which BoP customers live are very different to those of the conventional customer groups typically targeted by multinational companies. Also, the question as to whether the BoP population segment is already a market, or first needs to be developed, is under discussion. Consensus exists that the headcount potential and the total value of this market is large, albeit dispersed and difficult to address for companies.

The literature is still fragmented and lacks coherent and comprehensive concepts for a profitable business. The discussion on BoP evolved from seeing the segment purely as consumers to cooperation with the BoP, and finally to the need to include ethics and sustainability into the business approach. Still, much of the literature sees the "doing business at the BoP" as just a means to the end of poverty alleviation (inclusive business model, social business models). In this book the perspective is more straightforward: It investigates how multinational companies can actually create a profitable business model when addressing the BoP markets in SSA. Based on the findings of this chapter, the book will contribute to the academic and practical discussion around BoP in two ways:

1. It will focus on "how" to reach the BoP customer segment, which is the question about a working business model. The BoP conceptual logic will combine elements of BoP 1.0 and BoP 2.0 literature.
2. The analysis will broaden the empirical basis in BoP literature, which is still lacking, by conducting a qualitative empirical study with the aim to understand how multinational pharmaceutical companies manage to reach the BoP in Sub-Saharan Africa.

The following chapter will introduce the business model concept with a clear focus on the BoP context.

References

Agnihotri A (2012) Revisiting the debate over the bottom of the pyramid market. J Macromark 32:417–423

Ahmed FE (2013) The market at the bottom of the pyramid: understanding the culture of poverty. Perspect Glob Dev Technol 12:489–513

Akula V (2008) Business basics at the base of the pyramid. Harv Bus Rev 86:53–57

Ausrød VL, Sinha V, Widding Ø (2017) Business model design at the base of the pyramid. J Clean Prod 162:982–996

Banerjee A, Duflo E (2007) The economic lives of the poor. J Econ Perspect 21:141–167

Bendell J, Kearins K (2005) The political bottom line: the emerging dimension to corporate responsibility for sustainable development. Bus Strateg Environ 14:372–383

Bendul JC, Rosca E, Pivovarova D (2017) Sustainable supply chain models for base of the pyramid. J Clean Prod 162:107–120

Bonsu SK, Polsa P (2011) Governmentality at the base-of-the-pyramid. J Macromark 31:236–244

Borchardt M, Ndubisi NO, Jabbour CJC, Grebinevych O, Pereira GM (2019) The evolution of base of the pyramid approaches and the role of multinational and domestic business ventures: value-commitment and profit-making perspectives. Indus Market Manag. https://www.sciencedirect.com/science/article/abs/pii/S0019850119300574. Accessed 9 July 2020

Byerlee D, Janvry AD, Sadoulet E, Townsend R, Klytchnikova I (2007) World Development Report 2008. Agriculture for development. World Bank, Washington, DC

Calton JM, Werhane PH, Hartman LP, Bevan D (2013) Building partnerships to create social and economic value at the base of the global development pyramid. J Bus Ethics 117:721–733

Caneque FC, Hart SL (eds) (2015) Base of the Pyramid 3.0: Sustainable development through innovation and entrepreneurship. Routledge, Oxon

Chikweche T, Fletcher R (2012) Revisiting the marketing mix at the bottom of pyramid (BOP): from theoretical considerations to practical realities. J Consum Mark 29:507–520

Collier P (2007) The bottom billion: why the poorest countries are failing and what can be done about it. Oxford University Press, Oxford

de Soto H (2000) The mystery of capital: why capitalism triumphs in the west and fails everywhere else. Bantam Press, Berkshire

Dembek K, Sivasubramaniam N, Chmielewski DA (2019) A systematic review of the bottom/base of the pyramid literature: cumulative evidence and future directions. J Bus Ethics 1:1–18

Dolan C, Roll K (2013) ASR Forum: Engaging with African informal economies: Capital's new frontier: from "unusable" economies to bottom-of-the-pyramid markets in Africa. Afr Stud Rev 56:123–146

Dolfsma W, Duysters G, Costa I (eds) (2009) Multinationals and emerging economies: the quest for innovation and sustainability. Edward Elgar Publishing, Cheltenham

Galariotis E, Villa C, Yusupov N (2011) Recent advances in lending to the poor with asymmetric information. J Dev Stud 47:1371–1390

Gold S, Hahn R, Seuring S (2013) Sustainable supply chain management in "Base of the Pyramid" food projects—A path to triple bottom line approaches for multinationals? Int Bus Rev 22:784–799

Gupta V, Khilji SE (2013) Revisiting fortune at base of the pyramid (BoP). South Asian J Glob Bus Res 2:8–26

Hahn R (2009) The ethical rational of business for the poor – integrating the concepts bottom of the pyramid, sustainable development, and corporate citizenship. J Bus Ethics 84:313–324

Hammond AL, Kramer W (2007) The next 4 Billion: market size and business strategy at the base of the pyramid. World Resources Institute, Washington, DC

Hammond AL, Kramer WJ, Katz RS, Tran JT, Walker C (2007) The next 4 billion. Innov Technol Govern Global 2:147–158

Hart SL (2007) Capitalism at the crossroads: aligning business, earth, and humanity. Pearson Education, London

Hart SL, Christensen CM (2002) The great leap: driving innovation from the base of the pyramid. MIT Sloan Manag Rev 44:51

Holt T, Lahrichi M, Santos da Silva J (2015) Africa: a continent of opportunity for pharma and patients. https://www.mckinsey.com/industries/pharmaceuticals-and-medical-products/our-insights/africa-a-continent-of-opportunity-for-pharma-and-patients. Accessed 15 Jul 2018

Ireland J (2008) Lessons for successful BOP marketing from Caracas' slums. J Consum Mark 25:430–438

Jaiswal AK (2008) The fortune at the bottom or the middle of the pyramid? Innov Technol Govern Global 3:85–100

Janda SV, Hillebrand CM, Kuester S (eds) (2018) We are (not) all the same! A differentiated look at the BOP consumer market. American Marketing Association. https://www.ama.org/academics/Documents/2018%20Win. Accessed 20 Jan 2020

Jenkins R (2005) Globalization, corporate social responsibility and poverty. Int Aff 81:525–540

Johnson S (2007) SC Johnson builds business at the base of the pyramid. Glob Bus Organ Excell 26:6–17

Karamchandani A, Kubzansky M, Lalwani N (2011) Is the bottom of the pyramid really for you. Harv Bus Rev 89:107–111

Karnani A (2005) Misfortune at the Bottom of the Pyramid. Greener Manag Int 51:99–111

Karnani A (2007a) Doing well by doing good — Case study: 'Fair & Lovely' whitening cream. Strateg Manag J 28:1351–1357

Karnani A (2007b) The mirage of marketing to the bottom of the pyramid: how the private sector can help alleviate poverty. Calif Manag Rev 49:90–111

Klein M (2008) Poverty alleviation through sustainable strategic business models: essays on poverty alleviation as a business strategy. Dissertation, Erasmus Research Institute of Management (ERIM), Rotterdam

Kolk A, Rivera-Santos M, Rufín C (2014) Reviewing a decade of research on the "base/bottom of the pyramid" (BOP) concept. Bus Soc 53:338–377

Kowalkowski C, Witell L, Gustafsson A (2013) Any way goes: identifying value constellations for service infusion in SMEs. Bus Models 42:18–30

Kuo T, Hanafi J, Sun W, Robielos R (2016) The effects of national cultural traits on BOP consumer behavior. Sustainability 8:272ff

Kuttalam MG (2012) Micro-entrepreneurship: a sustenance tool in the unserved market. BIJIEMS 2:164–167

Landrum NE (2007) Advancing the "base of the pyramid" debate. Strateg Manag Rev 1:1–12

Lappeman J, Ransome K, Louw Z (2019) Not one segment: using global and local BoP characteristics to model country-specific consumer profiles. Eur Bus Rev 31:317–336

London T (2007a) A base-of-the-pyramid perspective on poverty alleviation. University of Michigan

London T (2007b) Connecting the rural poor to the world: Grameen's village phone in Bangladesh. William Davidson Institute/Michigan Ross School of Business. https://wdi-publishing.com/product/connecting-the-rural-poor-to-the-world-grameens-village-phone-in-bangladesh/. Accessed 28 Sep 2018

London T, Hart SL (2004) Reinventing strategies for emerging markets: beyond the transnational model. J Int Bus Stud 35:350–370

London T, Hart SL (2010) Next generation business strategies for the base of the pyramid: new approaches for building mutual value. Pearson Education, India

London T, Hart S (eds) (2011) Next generation business strategies for the base of the pyramid: new approaches for building mutual value. Pearson Education, Upper Saddle River, NJ

London T, Anupindi R, Sheth S (2010) Creating mutual value: lessons learned from ventures serving base of the pyramid producers. J Bus Res 63:582–594

Mohr J, Sengupta S, Slater SF (2012) Serving base-of-the-pyramid markets: meeting real needs through a customized approach. J Bus Strateg 33:4–14

Nagarajan G (2006) Unilever in India: Rural marketing initiative: marketing mastermind. The ICFAI University Press, p 75ff

Nagy M, Bennett D, Graham C (2019) Why include the BOP in your international marketing strategy. Int Mark Rev 37:76–97

Nakata C (2012) From the Special Issue Editor: Creating new products and services for and with the base of the pyramid. J Prod Innov Manag 29:3–5

Narayan D, Chambers R, Shah M, Petesch P (2000) Voices of the poor. Crying out for change. Oxford University Press for the World Bank

Novogratz J (2007) Meeting urgent needs with patient capital. Innov Technol Govern Global 2:19–30

Olsen M, Boxenbaum E (2009) Bottom-of-the-pyramid: organizational barriers to implementation. Calif Manag Rev 51:100–125

Omar M, Williams RL, Ensor J (2011) Sourcing or selling: the value flame at the base of the pyramid. Mark Intell Plan 29:233–246

Porter ME, Kramer MR, Zadek S (2007) Redefining corporate social responsibility. Harv Bus Rev 1:2007ff

Prahalad CK (2005) The fortune at the bottom of the pyramid: eradicating poverty through profits – Book review. Vikalpa 30:149–154

Prahalad CK (2006) The fortune at the bottom of the pyramid: eradicating poverty through profits. Wharton School Publishing, Upper Saddle River, NJ

Prahalad CK (2012) Bottom of the pyramid as a source of breakthrough innovations. J Prod Innov Manag 29:6–12

Prahalad CK, Hammond AL (2002) Serving the world's poor, profitably. Harv Bus Rev 80:48–59

Prahalad CK, Hammond AL (2004) Selling to the poor. Foreign Policy 142:30–37

Prahalad CK, Hart SL (1999) Strategies for the bottom of the pyramid: creating sustainable development. Ann Arbor. https://www.researchgate.net/profile/Stuart_Hart4/publication/268425222_Strategies_for_the_Bottom_of_the_Pyramid_Creating_Sustainable_Development/links/555b2b3508aeaaff3bfc0f66/Strategies-for-the-Bottom-of-the-Pyramid-Creating-Sustainable-Development.pdf. Accessed 18 Aug 2019

Prahalad CK, Hart SL (2002) The fortune at the bottom of the pyramid. Strat Bus 26:2–14

Ramachandran J, Pant A, Pani SK (2012) Building the BoP producer ecosystem: the evolving engagement of Fabindia with Indian Handloom Artisans. J Prod Innov Manag 29:33–51

Rangan VK, Chu M, Petkoski D (2011) The globe: segmenting the base of the pyramid. Harv Bus Rev 89:113–117
Rashid AT, Rahman M (2009) Making profit to solve development problems: the case of Telenor AS and the Village Phone Programme in Bangladesh. J Mark Manag 25:1049–1060
Rollert JP (2011) Does the top really support the bottom?—Adam Smith and the problem of the commercial pyramid. Bus Soc Rev 116:193–211
Sachs J, McArthur J, Schmidt-Traub G, Kruk M, Bahadur C, Faye M, McCord G (2004) Ending Africa's poverty trap. Brook Pap Econ Act 35:117–240
Schuster T, Holtbrügge D (2012) Market entry of multinational companies in markets at the bottom of the pyramid: a learning perspective. Int Bus Rev 21:817–830
Schuster T, Holtbrügge D (2014) Resource dependency, innovative strategies, and firm performance in BOP markets. J Prod Innov Manag 31:43–59
Sheth JN (2011) Impact of emerging markets on marketing: rethinking existing perspectives and practices. J Mark 75:166–182
Simanis E (2011) Needs, needs, everywhere, but not a BoP market to tap. In: London T, Hart S (eds) Next generation business strategies for the base of the pyramid. Financial Times Press, Upper Saddle River, NJ, pp 103–126
Simanis E (2013) Bringing bottom of the pyramid into business focus. In: Genevey R, Pachauri RK, Tubiana L (eds) Reducing inequalities: a sustainable development challenge. pp 217–232
Simanis E, Hart S, Duke D (2008) The base of the pyramid protocol: beyond "basic needs" business strategies. Innov Technol Govern Global 3:57–84
Sinkovics N, Sinkovics RR, Yamin M (2014) The role of social value creation in business model formulation at the bottom of the pyramid – implications for MNEs? Int Bus Rev 23:692–707
Subrahmanyan S, Gomez-Arias T (2008) Integrated approach to understanding consumer behavior at bottom of pyramid. J Consum Mark 25:402–412
Tarafdar M, Anekal P, Singh R (2011) Market development at the bottom of the pyramid: examining the role of information and communication technologies. Inf Technol Dev 18:311–331
Tashman P, Marano V (2010) Dynamic capabilities and base of the pyramid business strategies. J Bus Ethics 89:495–514
Tata R, Hart SL, Sharma A, Sarkar C (2013) Why making money is not enough. MIT Sloan Manag Rev 54:95–96
UNDP (2005) Human development report 2005: international cooperation at a crossroads: aid, trade and security in an unequal world. Human development report. Oxford University Press, New York
UNDP (2013) Realizing Africa's wealth: building inclusive business for shared prosperity. A UNDP African Facility for Inclusive Markets Report. New York
Vachani S, Smith NC (2008) Socially responsible distribution: distribution strategies for reaching the bottom of the pyramid. Calif Manag Rev 50:52–84
van der Klein W, Mancheron H, Wertheim-Heck S, Collée L (2012) BoP insights. Inclusive marketing research. Insights and key lessons from three pilots for pro-poor innovation
van der Merwe MD, Grobbelaar SS, Schutte CSL, von Leipzig KH (2017) The base of the pyramid: towards a high growth framework for SME action. IAMOT 2017 conference proceedings. International association for management of technology
Warnholz J-L (2007) Poverty reduction for profit? A critical examination of business opportunities at the Bottom of the Pyramid. QEH Working Paper Series
Whitehead M, Dahlgren G, Evans T (2001) Equity and health sector reforms: can low-income countries escape the medical poverty trap? Lancet 358:833–836

Chapter 3
Business Models in the Bottom of the Pyramid Context

How can one generate profit while improving the situation of the BoP population? This question and the various economic opportunities at the BoP have pointed researchers and practitioners toward a systematic investigation of business models in the context of the BoP. As BoP markets exhibit divergent income structures and distribution systems compared to high-income and developed markets they require new business approaches (Dodgson et al. 2014; Ricart et al. 2004). In their study on product deployment in low-income countries, Chesbrough et al. (2006) emphasize that successful companies are those that have developed the "right" business model for the BoP market. However, the business model in the BoP literature is still considered something of a mystery. Seelos (2010) criticizes that research on business models in the BoP context combines a free mix of elements of stakeholder theory, institutional theory, contingency theory, resource dependency theory, and others. Articles on the subject (Bocken et al. 2014; Boons and Lüdeke-Freund 2013) contain several narrative elements but leave unresolved how business model elements are chosen, for what purpose, and what lessons can be learned from these examples. There is still no consensus on how resources at the BoP need to be configured in order to create value since few organizational templates exist (Seelos 2010).

This chapter starts with a brief overview of the general business model literature in order to create a basic common understanding. The next section will discuss business model development for the BoP target group before focussing on the success factors and challenges when addressing the BoP market.

3.1 The Business Model Concept in Literature

In the past 15 years, the business model idea attracted the attention of managers and academics alike. Initially, the term was regularly employed in management literature and described the "way companies earn their money." Indeed, company operations have always followed an industry-specific logic, but it is only recently that a holistic

P. von Carlowitz, *Success in the Bottom of the Pyramid Market in Africa*,
SpringerBriefs in Business, https://doi.org/10.1007/978-3-030-59068-0_3

approach has developed that tries to explain the value creation logic behind a business approach. Fostered by the emergence of the internet and e-commerce the business model attracted the increasing attention of researchers in the 1990s (Dodgson et al. 2014; Verstraete and Jouison 2007).

In principle:

> A business model comprises the combined elements of 'who', 'what', 'when', 'why', 'where', 'how' and 'how much' involved in providing customers and end users with products and services. (Mitchell and Coles 2003)

Based on these fundamental questions on how a business approach works end-to-end, researchers agree that a business model is a new unit of analysis (Zott et al. 2011). Different authors such as Osterwalder (2005a, 2010), Zott et al. (2011), and Stewart and Zhao (2000) have conducted extensive research and have worked on the development of the theory of business models. A wide range of definitions of the term business model exists. Authors refer to a business model as a statement of how the business works (Stewart and Zhao 2000), a representation (Morris et al. 2005), an architecture (Dubosson-Torbay et al. 2002), a method of doing business (Zott et al. 2011), a configuration (Gummesson et al. 2010; Chesbrough and Rosenbloom 2002), or a conceptual model (Osterwalder et al. 2005a). This variety of understanding gives rise to different definitions. The major ones are summarized in Table 3.1.

It is apparent that academics have different angles on what a business model is as they highlight different aspects. Some common key elements can be identified despite these different perspectives: *Value proposition* (Casadesus-Masanell and Ricart 2010; Chesbrough 2010; Johnson et al. 2008; Magretta 2002; Morris et al. 2005; Osterwalder and Pigneur 2010; Teece 2010), *customer segment* (Chesbrough 2010; Morris et al. 2005; Osterwalder and Pigneur 2010), *profit formula* considering the revenue streams and costs related to the business model (Casadesus-Masanell and Ricart 2010; Chesbrough 2010; Gassmann et al. 2013; Johnson et al. 2008; Morris et al. 2005; Osterwalder and Pigneur 2010; Teece 2010), as well as the key resources and processes needed to make the business model work (Casadesus-Masanell and Ricart 2010; Gassmann et al. 2013; Johnson et al. 2008; Osterwalder and Pigneur 2010).

Zott et al. (2011) criticize this lack of definitional accuracy, which inhibits a convergence of perspectives and leads to a multitude of possible interpretations. The authors argue that the term "business model" has been used to address different research questions in different contexts leading to the evolution of different literature streams (Zott and Amit 2010). Authors divide the literature into three broad categories, which are not exhaustive:

1. There is a focus on the internet, e-business, and the use of information technology (Dodgson et al. 2014; Osterwalder et al. 2005a). Through the recent advances in information and communication technologies (ICT), this stream has received the greatest attention so far (Zott et al. 2011). The emergence of the internet has opened up new possibilities when it comes to how to do business, both within and across company and industry boundaries. This, in turn, has nurtured the

Table 3.1 Selected business model definitions

Author	Definition
Timmers (1998, p. 2)	[. . .] an *architecture* of the product, service and information flows, including a description of the various business actors and their roles; a description of the potential benefits for the various business actors; a description of the sources of revenues.
Amit and Zott (2001, p. 493)	A business model depicts the *design* of transaction content, structure, and governance so as to create value through the exploitation of business opportunities.
Hamel (2001, p. 10)	[...] the major *components of a business model*: customer interface, core strategy, strategic resources, and value network. These basic components are linked by three "*bridging*" *components*: customer benefits, configuration of activities, and company boundaries.
Chesbrough and Rosenbloom (2002, p. 529)	[. . .] the *heuristic logic* that connects technical potential with the realization of economic value.
Magretta (2002, p. 4)	[...] *Stories that explain how enterprises work.* A good business model answers Peter Drucker's old question: Who is the customer? And what does the customer value? It also answers the fundamental questions every manager must ask: How do we make money in this business? What is the underlying economic logic that explains how we can deliver value to customers at an appropriate cost?
Morris et al. (2005, p. 72)	[...] *Concise representation* of how an interrelated set of decision variables in the areas of venture strategy, architecture, and economics are addressed to create sustainable competitive advantage in defined markets. It has six fundamental components: Value proposition, customer, internal processes, external positioning, economic model, and personal/investor factors.
Johnson et al. (2008, p. 60)	A business model, from our point of view, consists of four *interlocking elements* that, taken together, create and deliver value. The most important to get right, by far, is the first.
Cassadesus-Masanell and Ricart (2010, p. 195)	A reflection of the firm's *realized strategy*.
Teece (2010, p. 173)	A business model articulates the *logic* and provides data and other evidence that demonstrates how a business creates and delivers value to customers. It also outlines the *architecture* of revenues, costs, and profits associated with the business enterprise delivering that value.
Osterwalder and Pigneur (2010, p. 14)	A business model describes the *rationale* of how an organization creates, delivers, and captures value.
Zott and Amit (2013, p. 404)	The business model describes the *system of interdependent activities* that are performed by the firm and by its partners and the mechanisms that link these activities to each other [...]. A business model is thus a template that depicts the way the firm conducts its business.
Schallmo (2013, p. 16)	A business model is the *fundamental logic* of a company that describes which value in which way is created for the customer and partner. A business model answers the question, how the created value will flow back to companies in the form of revenues.

Source: Own illustration

development of the literature on what is termed *digital business models* (Dubosson-Torbay et al. 2002; Magretta 2002; Mahadevan 2000; Yip 2004).
2. Another part of business model research deals with innovation and technology management (Kuriyan et al. 2008; Zott et al. 2011). Much of this literature is devoted to the question of how firms can commercialize their new technologies and ideas through business models (Chesbrough and Rosenbloom 2002; Miles et al. 2006). According to this more functionalist perspective, the business model is regarded as the financial and organizational architecture that connects a firm's resources to market outcomes (Teece 2010). Hence, the business model is seen as a facilitator of technological innovation and commercialization.
3. A growing amount of research sees the business model itself as the subject of innovation (Mitchell and Coles 2003; Zott et al. 2011). Especially business practitioners and consultants focus their studies on business model innovation and the implications for business model design (Foss and Saebi 2014). For instance, IBM Global Business Services interviewed 765 leaders from public and private enterprises worldwide and revealed that financially outperforming firms had put twice as much emphasis on business model innovation as had underperformers (IBM Global Business Services 2006). In literature, researchers and business practitioners are interested in gaining new insights into the nature of value creation (Goyal et al. 2014; Gummesson et al. 2010), the relationship between a business model and company performance (Zott and Amit 2008), and the distinction between the business model and strategy concepts (Goethals 2011).

In order to operationalize the conceptual discussion and make the business model usable for practitioners, the structure of the business model for the BoP discussion in this book will follow Gassmann et al. (2013). They have developed a simple, yet holistic, model for describing a business model through its individual elements. This model consists of four elements that supplement and encompass the definitional elements of business models:

1. The *customer,* who always stands at the center of all business models. In this book, it is the BoP customer in Sub-Saharan Africa (see Sect. 2.2).
2. The *value proposition* describes a company's scope of offering that satisfies some customer needs. This can be either by solving a challenge/problem (pain reliever) or adding to something positive from the customer's perspective (gain creator).
3. The *value generation* includes supply-side activities of the value chain such as using resources, capabilities, and processes to create the offering (*value creation*). It also comprises the sales-side activities on how the offering is delivered to the customer (*value delivery*) (Osterwalder et al. 2005a; Osterwalder and Pigneur 2010; Zott et al. 2011; Teece 2010).[1]

[1]For the purpose of consistency, the logic of the book will follow the broad definition of *value generation* but within the section differentiates between *value delivery* and *value creation*.

4. The term *value capture* (also referred to as *revenue model, profit formula)* refers to the mechanics of how companies capture value for themselves through their business activities, hence, how the revenue model (Gassmann et al. 2013) or profit equation (Johnson et al. 2008) works. It covers revenue generation and costs.

As a consequence, the understanding of business models in this book is that of a *holistic concept* of how business activities interact in an interdependent system in order to profitably serve the targeted customer segment. It shows how an organization *generates* (*creates and delivers*) and *captures* value from the targeted customer segment with the use of a *network of partners* (Osterwalder et al. 2005b; Osterwalder et al. 2010; Zott et al. 2011).

Before addressing the specifics of business models for the BoP market segments, the need to adapt, or to even innovate, a company's business model is briefly discussed. This research field—as mentioned above—is important when establishing the BoP context for business model analysis and development. In principle, business model innovation occurs when innovation is not geared toward a product or process innovation but rather toward the entire approach of doing business (the business model) (Breitenmoser 2015). The focus lies on generating new sales potential via a new business approach. This can be achieved by creating new value propositions for (new) customers and generating value to suppliers and business partners, allowing the company to capture additional value with its new approach (Casadesus-Masanell and Zhu 2013). The triggers for business model innovation can either be internal or external to the company: Teece (2010) argues that a successful business model must always be seen in the specific business environment/ecosystem in which it operates. It is also linked to the development of strategies and helps to generate a sustainable competitive advantage. Business model innovation only results in a sustainable competitive advantage if it is hard to imitate, or copying is not economical for competitors (e.g., harming existing partnerships, unable to scale the business model as the second mover) (Casadesus-Masanell and Zhu 2013). In addition, authors have argued that focusing on specific capabilities can induce business model innovation (Battistella et al. 2017) as much as changes in portfolio (through innovation or acquisition) (Giesen et al. 2010). However, there is usually an inherent resistance to change within companies, especially when their current business model is successful (Buliga et al. 2015).

Authors (Giesen et al. 2007; Clauss 2016) have differentiated between three types of business model innovation: First, innovation in an industry's value chain that changes the "rules of the game" and can actually lead to the definition of a new (sub-) industry. Second, a change in the company's operating model and a change in organizational structure. Third, reconfiguration of revenue models/value capture which can, for instance, result from digitalization. This is often based on new value propositions or changes to pricing models. Thus, changes that lead to adjusted business models are frequently related to value-generating activities, that is, performing new activities, reconfiguration of capabilities and resources, or a new distribution of tasks within the partner network (e.g., outsourcing of production)

(Amit and Zott 2012). Bowien (2015) points out that a changed value proposition in an extended business ecosystem is a frequent result of a business model innovation.

Going forward in the analysis, multinational pharmaceutical companies look at business model adaptation/innovation when addressing the BoP in Sub-Saharan Africa. Addressing African consumers is, for many multinational companies, already a stretch of existing business models, which are usually designed for developed market structures. Going one step further and setting up a business in the BoP market segments is a new territory for international companies. The firms are entering a widely unknown business ecosystem in which the roles of stakeholders are not yet cast in stone. This calls for new ideas and approaches on how to create a profitable business. The next chapter will, therefore, look at what the specifics are when developing a business model for the BoP market segment before turning to success factors and challenges.

3.2 Developing Business Models at the Bottom of the Pyramid

A great proportion of the literature on business models for the BoP deals with social or sustainable business ventures. These are created and defined by addressing a social or sustainability-related problem while being financially self-sustainable. Profits realized by the business are reinvested in the business itself (or used to start other social businesses) with the aim of increasing social impact, for example, expanding the company's reach, improving the products or services, or in other ways subsidizing the social mission (Yunus et al. 2010). However, while social missions can underpin social value creation there is no clear differentiation between social entrepreneurship and business entrepreneurship at the BoP. This is because both derive their justification from the management of (social) grievances. With or without a social focus, the literature tries to explain how the dilemma of this so-called double bottom line (making a social and economic profit) can be resolved. How can one generate profit while reducing poverty or overcoming other social challenges that can be found at the BoP?

This chapter will provide an overview of the most important aspects found in the literature on business models in the BoP context. This serves as a basis for the empirical analysis in Chap. 6, which discusses possibilities for multinational pharmaceutical companies to draw up profitable business models for the BoP markets in Sub-Saharan Africa.

3.2.1 *Value Proposition*

The value proposition explains which products or services are offered to the BoP community and what value they offer to the customer. People at the BoP are looking for affordable products and services that solve their problems (so-called pain relievers) or improve their situation, for instance, providing access to important products such as medication (so-called gain creators) (Jose 2008). A prerequisite condition to meet these expectations is to offer tailored solutions accounting for customer needs and the business conditions found at the BoP. For example, to create a better cooking stove for rural women in India, the company *First Energy* observed local women's cooking habits for a long time in order to understand their customs. Then they tailored the stove's design and features in ways that perfectly suited the local cooking routine and created a benefit for the women. *First Energy* was able to sell a million units within 5 years (Chu 2007; Sánchez and Schmid 2013). Also, buyers need to know what the product is and does (Sánchez and Schmid 2013; Shukla and Bairiganjan 2011). If people do not know how to use the new stove or that it can save money and time or that it has other useful and convincing benefits they will not buy it (Bloom and Chatterji 2009). Thus, one product feature for the BoP is often an easy-to-use design and efficient communication about the benefits of the (unknown) product (i.e., promotion). After examining several business models that target the BoP, researchers concluded that a "social mission" is not a necessary prerequisite to generate social value as this is usually one outcome of business at the BoP (Sinkovics et al. 2014). This is inherent in the value proposition/business model approach of creating value for the target customer group, here the BoP segment. Even if the motive of a business model targeting the BoP market is for-profit, it is normally compatible with a social benefit and consistent with the double bottom line. The difference between a for-profit and a social enterprise is the primary goal: In a for-profit business model the social benefit for the BoP might not be maximized as it would be in an inclusive business model where social targets have priority, and the approach's focus is on BoP constraints with great social implications.

In order to generate a strong and relevant value proposition, London et al. (2010) recommend investigating the constraints that BoP consumers, producers, and entrepreneurs face. Authors differentiate between constraints that affect productivity/value creation and value delivery/value capture. Sinkovics et al. (2014) extend the model by adding trigger constraints that are of a general nature but which also affect the BoP population (Table 3.2). Companies can design an efficient and targeted value proposition and business model around any of the constraints.

Table 3.2 shows typical constraints relevant in the BoP market. This is not to say that many of them are not also constraints for market players in general, especially in emerging markets. Some of the constraints are, however, more specific to BoP stakeholders, such as the lack of education, no access to insurance, and exploitation by middlemen. It is apparent that there are many constraints that a value proposition can address. Those constraints describe the situation faced by BoP customers. This in turn determines the needs and requirements of customers that companies'

Table 3.2 Constraints at the bottom of the pyramid

Constraints ("Pains") faced by BoP	Type of constraint	Example
General constraints	Changed industry conditions	– Diminishing competitive advantage
	Act of God	– Drought
		– Destruction due to natural disaster
	Sociocultural factors	– Unemployment
		– Immobility
		– Illiteracy
	Social constraints	– Injustice
		– Exploitation
		– Lack of employment opportunities
		– Corruption
Productivity/value creation	Input resources	– Lack of access to high-quality material
		– Low quality of local material
		– Supplier power to drive price and quantity
	Financial resources	– Lack of working and investment capital
		– Exploitation by extra-legal lenders
		– No access to insurance
	Production resources	– Inadequate or lacking technology
		– Lack of equipment and infrastructure
		– Lack of expertise and know-how
		– Lack of education (technical, business, and industry-related)
		– Storage space
		– Underdeveloped human resources
Value delivery/value capture	Market access	– Poor infrastructure (communication, transportation)
		– Lack of awareness of market expectations
		– Inability to meet market expectations
		– No market awareness of the firm's offering
		– Export barriers
		– Market skepticism
		– Community acceptance/legitimacy
	Market power	– No capacity to link directly with buyers
		– Lack of direct access to end markets
		– Exploitation by middlemen
	Market security	– Lack of consistent buyers
		– Price fluctuation
		– Crime and insecurity
		– Lack of government assistance
		– Bureaucracy, corruption

Source: Own illustration, based on Sinkovics et al. (2014)

offerings need to satisfy. A value proposition—and thus a firm's offering—need not address all pain points or the above mentioned constraints. It should focus on the most urgent needs and those that can be satisfied given the firm's capabilities and resources to ensure efficient value generation. Due to the specific nature and large number of constraints/needs at the BoP and the lack of knowledge and experience of MNCs, some authors see a key success factor in developing the business model on site. Only then is it possible to identify and to deal with the relevant constraints faced by the companies (Hammond and Kramer 2007; Mason and Chakrabarti 2017). Besides these constraints being a key part of value proposition definition, some of them feature in the other elements of the business model, namely value generation and capture.

3.2.2 Value Generation: Creation and Delivery

Value is generated through a value-creating system (value chain) in which different stakeholders (suppliers, business partners, customers, etc.) cooperate. It describes how value is created and how the offer is delivered to the target customer group. This not only involves the internal value chain but also affected actions within the extended network of suppliers and partners. Both business model elements have to fit together and should adapt to the BoP customers' constraints and opportunities in order to generate a profitable outcome (Budinich et al. 2007).

As constraints and challenges of the market play a pivotal role in the design of a suitable business model, Parmigiani and Rivera-Santos (2015) constructed a framework that shows how these institutional restrictions impact the different value generation steps in a poverty context. In doing so, they focus on institutional voids which are defined as a failure of most governments in Emerging Markets "… in providing the institutions necessary to support basic business operations" (Khanna and Palepu 1997). This translates into a challenging business environment that has effects along the company's value chain, and hence impacts the entire value generation system (see Fig. 3.1).

Most of the voids shown are relevant for emerging markets in general and not only for the BoP segment. However, as Parmigiani and Rivera-Santos (2015) argue, they are more pronounced in the BoP segment which, to a great extent, corresponds to the informal economy. This, for instance, makes enforcing a contract more difficult, especially if it is not common to have a written contract in the first place. Another example is the lack of skilled labor, which is especially pronounced among the BoP population where general education levels are typically below the national level as school fees are too expensive for the poor.

The voids mentioned in Fig. 3.1 need to be dealt with by companies addressing the BoP customer segment when drawing up a functioning business model. Business routines of a company in developed and high-income markets are unlikely to work (in the same way as) in the BoP environment. In marketing and sales, companies use Word-of-Mouth and Door-to-Door approaches. They also collaborate with NGOs in

Institutional Voids and Challenges: Fields	Raw Material Procurement	Manufacturing and Operations	Distribution and Logistics	Marketing and Sales
Product Market Difficult to assess product attributes, esp. quality due to information asymmetries	Difficulty in finding good suppliers and acceptable quality, as there is a lack of certification and industry standards			Difficulty to communicate with customers, understand their needs, promote a value proposition, and establish a brand
Labor Market Limited availability of skills and knowledge		The scarcity of skilled employees, due to low education levels and poor training	Difficulty in finding, training, and motivating qualified individuals to act as distributors	
Capital Market Limited availability of financial options		Difficulty in financing plant construction and equipment due to poor debt and equity market		
Contracting Difficult to create a written contract that can be enforced	Difficult to guarantee long-term material flows		Difficult to set up, enforce, and end agreements	Difficult to work with retailers to ensure pricing, promotion, and prompt payments
Regulatory Difficult to plan based on a stable regulatory climate and political regime		Difficult to address corruption, ambiguous regulations, and changing government policies		

Fig. 3.1 Effects of institutional challenges along the value chain. Source: Own illustration, based on Parmigiani and Rivera-Santos (2015)

the area of education and distribution. The issue of written contract as a basis for business is often switched to more informal agreements based on trust (Parmigiani and Rivera-Santos 2015). Companies successfully addressing the BoP market find new, unconventional ways along the entire value chain to deal with the institutional voids and overcome business challenges. In her study Arnold (2018) finds that building a network and taking an inclusive value creation approach is key for success in any BoP venture undertaken by a multinational company. For this reason, multinational companies need to localize in order to develop cultural skills and create local partnerships.

Constraints have an impact on the value generation process along the entire value chain just as they have a direct influence on the value proposition development, as shown. Organizations need to keep in mind that value creation systems are subject to dynamics—an ever-changing business environment that is shaped by uncertainty. Therefore, value chain activities must often be reconfigured, reduced, eliminated, or re-invented if they are to work and be successful (Chan Kim and Mauborgne 2005). Thus, firms need to develop and acquire new (and specific) resources to succeed at the BoP (Schuster and Holtbrügge 2014). This calls for business model innovation as will be discussed below.

3.2.3 Value Capture and Revenue Model

As described above, business models at the BoP usually have a double bottom line with social and economic profit as a goal. "Mutual value" is about creating value for the BoP while simultaneously creating value for the ventures themselves (London 2007). The economic profit equation describes the value captured from the revenues generated through sales, how costs are structured, and how capital is employed in the value creation system. The social profit equation describes the social profit and/or the environmental profit achieved through the BoP business. This could be the reduction of poverty, pollution, or other factors negatively affecting the environment and the people that live at the BoP. Here the core difference between social business ventures and for-profit business models becomes apparent: On the one hand, a social business' profit equation targets the full recovery of costs and the maximization of social profit. For-profit organizations, on the other hand, usually target the maximization of current and prospective economic profit while the importance of the social profit varies and is secondary. In both cases, both equations are important. Ventures are expected to generate acceptable economic returns to their investors and provide valued societal returns to the local community in which they operate (Hart and Milstein 2003; London and Hart 2004).

In general, when drawing up the revenue model the living conditions of BoP customers and the relevant business ecosystem need to be considered, e.g., low income, limited cash flow, limited access to credit, etc. In order to capture the value as a company, the cost side must be included in the consideration. The key is to find ways to cut costs across all elements of the value generation activities of the business model. An alternative is to find a new way of doing business that is more cost-efficient. Only then will the company manage to capture value (that is, make a profit) despite low price levels at the BoP.

3.2.4 Business Model Innovation and Adaptation for BoP Markets

Prahalad (2006) proposes to find this "fortune at the Bottom of the Pyramid" through business model innovation since the structure of the BoP market is different from that of high-income markets. Due to the dynamic BoP environment, Schallmo et al. (2012) highlight the need to permanently evaluate the dynamics in the target market and within the company in order to reconcile the compatibility of the business model with the (changed) internal and external conditions so as to ensure lasting success. This notion of business model innovation also applies when multinational companies expand their market reach into the BoP segment.

Business model innovation requires MNCs to redesign products or services, distribution models, and entire value chains in order for each of them to cater to the specific needs and market mechanisms at the BoP. It is about innovation within a clearly defined opportunity space that consists of considerations of cost, quality, sustainable development, local knowledge, specific needs, and large volumes (Prahalad and Hart 2000). Doing business at the BoP requires extensive operational and organizational change. Therefore, the business model framework for the BoP segment has to answer how to (re-)organize value generation in the BoP environmental context. Only then will it be able to create value for the customer and to capture value for the company.

While the previous sections focused on developing new business models to deal with the specifics and special constraints of the BoP markets, Seelos and Mair (2007) propose a different approach: Rather than developing completely new business models it can be sensible to assemble different building blocks into a new overall business model that is capable of profitably reaching the poor. What they are basically suggesting is a business model adaptation, if not innovation (Simanis and Duke 2014). They provide some practical points helping to innovate/adapt a business model (Table 3.3).

3.3 Success Factors of Business Models in the Bottom of the Pyramid Market

The importance of addressing BoP consumers differently to consumers at the top of the income pyramid has been stressed (GIZ 2012; Gradl and Knobloch 2010; UNDP 2013, 2014). The question is which elements of the operational business approach

Table 3.3 Business model innovation activities to address the BoP market

Business model innovation-related activities for success in the BoP market	Rationale
Scan geographic areas of interest for organizations with business models that aim to serve the poor.	Number and types of organizations may indicate important aspects of the environment (e.g., homogeneity of culture or language)
Gain an understanding of goal-setting, strategy, culture, structure of local organizations.	Size, scope, longevity, and strategic fit can be attributes that help to identify organizations that can be potential partners.
Establish relationships with local organizations from the beginning.	Work on gaining the trust of potential partner organizations by learning to speak their language and respecting their identity. Help to build up scale and scope; build mutual trust in partner intentions and competencies.
Identify relevant bottlenecks in order to build the business model around the constraining element.	Providing capacity to an existing model eliminates managerial complexity and provides for an easy interface between partners; the centrality of the bottleneck element to the business models of both partners aligns intentions and enables easy performance measures.
Start the business model design by thinking about replicating your existing competencies to support market development in foreign countries or redeploying competencies by existing country organizations to build new product markets.	Existing capabilities allow faster time to market and eliminate complexity and uncertainty; they naturally fit higher-income customers, enabling revenues to be generated while efficiently eliminating the bottleneck in your partner's strategy.
Ensure that the business model includes an income-increase-logic for the people at the BoP.	Income increase improves the ability of the poor to make consumption choices, and at the same time, expand your own customer base.
Observe and track the market dynamic, the own business performance and strategic objectives.	Recognize and address emerging threats, evaluate the possibility of building relationship-specific assets or asset configurations.

Source: Based on Seelos and Mair (2007)

(business model) need to be adjusted to the needs and circumstances of the BoP customers. What are the key success factors leading to a profitable business model for the BoP?

When practitioners gained their first experience in doing business in the BoP segment, they found it difficult to apply general business model implications. Thus, many researchers turned to investigating success factors that should be considered when doing business in BoP markets (Habib and Zurawicki 2010; Simanis et al. 2005). Over the years, a comprehensive number of studies has been conducted investigating and identifying critical success factors in BoP markets (Table 3.4).

The success factors described in literature for business model development in the BoP market can be summed up as follows: The single most frequently mentioned success factor in the papers quoted is finding the appropriate product or offering (with the right packaging) at an affordable price (third most frequently named success factor). Related, and also frequently named, is the clear focus on BoP customers and to understand their needs. Both relate to the idea of finding an

Table 3.4 Success factors for business in the BoP market in literature

Success factors	Title of article	Author
– Designing the right products – Stretching the purchasing power – Micro-financing and warranties	The bottom of the pyramid: Key roles for businesses	Habib and Zurawicki (2010)
– Localize base product – Bundle products – Offer enabling service (engage customers, provide needed skills) – Cultivate customer peer groups	Reality Check at the Bottom of the Pyramid	Simanis (2012)
– Design for sustainability – New technologies and new sociocultural meanings – Human-centered design for co-creation	Design Considerations for Base of the Pyramid (BoP) Projects	Castillo et al. (2012)
– Innovate offering for wellbeing of BoP – Reduce costs and provide microcredits – Long-term focus and investment – Alliances with NGOs, government and local BoP firms	Tapping into the Bottom of the Pyramid (BoP) Market in South Africa: Possible? And how?	Oodith and Parumasur (2013)
– Community benefit model – Collaborative value partnerships – Leverage on global strengths – Local resource sharing	The Concept of Cockroach Theory of Sustainable and Scalable Organizational and Individual Growth	Raj and Aithal (2018)
– Affordable price – Functionality of products – Service specialization – Flexible payment systems – Training and employment of BoP community – Network building – Scaling up of target segments	Critical Factors for Success among Social Enterprises in India	Matsumoto (2018)

Source: Own illustration

effective value proposition for which transparency of customer needs is required. Success factors relevant to value delivery that are mentioned are promotion/marketing and distribution. However, they are less frequently referenced in the literature reviewed. Also, among the top named success factors is the localization of activities and having a strong partner network, which are both aspects of the "value creation" side of a business model. The remaining factors in the list are only referred to by a few authors and do not seem to be as relevant as the ones discussed.

Some early authors (Prahalad 2006; Hammond et al. 2007; Prahalad and Hammond 2004) came up with the idea that products and services for the BoP have to be based on the "three As," to meet the needs of BoP consumers: affordability, accessibility, and availability. This was extended to a fourth "A," namely awareness, in a paper by Anderson and Markides (2007) and the paper by Anderson (2006). The aforementioned *4 As-Model* covers many of the success factors discussed in the literature:

Affordability is a key success factor as BoP customers are price sensitive. One way to lower the price is to sell the offering in smaller packages that are more in line with the limited cash flow of consumers.[2] Alternatively, it is feasible to cooperate with microcredit institutions to overcome the barrier of high upfront investment. In some industries, it is vital to achieve economies of scale to reduce per-unit-cost and prices. In other industries the lever is product development, pursuing a design-to-cost approach.

Accessibility is about reaching the BoP. Taking restrictions (e.g., the high cost of traveling to the nearest store/service point) faced by the BoP population into account and thus ensuring BoP access to the offering is a success factor. It includes the distribution approach which is linked to the next point, namely availability.

Availability of the offering refers to production and logistics. It is about ensuring the supply of the products to the customers. This can be achieved, for instance, by partnering with local producers, distributors, or running an on-site storage facility. Partnering can be informal or more formal along the lines of a franchise system (Chikweche and Fletcher 2011). Alternatively, individuals can be empowered as entrepreneurs for last-mile distribution (Bendul et al. 2017). In some cases, new technologies may help to increase availability, e.g., in telecommunication over-the-air recharging of pre-paid mobile tariffs and efficiency increases in storage management.

Awareness is about making BoP customers aware of the offering. It is related to market development and promotion. Awareness may be created by using existing networks such as the (distribution) partner structure and sales outlets to introduce the offering to consumers. Training all stakeholders can also enhance the effectiveness of awareness creation.

The 4 As model captures very relevant success factors and many of the criteria in Table 3.4 can be related to one of the "As." Analyzing four case studies, Chikweche and Fletcher (2012) find especially availability and affordability to be of great importance.

In a similar manner, Gebauer et al. (2017) suggest successful business models need to be re-invented or newly designed specifically for the BoP market. They should feature the following success factors:

1. *Inclusiveness*

   Inclusiveness aims to address the difficult BoP market characteristics that usually describe it by involving the poor in the business model and taking them beyond the sole role of customers. This is in line with the BoP 2.0 concept discussed in Sect. 2.3. On the one hand, this means integrating the poor as clients on the demand side, supplying them with affordable products or services. Typical

[2] Karnani (2007) pointed out that selling in smaller packages with a higher profit is not actually increasing affordability as the overall price for comparable volumes is much higher. Nonetheless, if affordability is interpreted as "being able to buy a product at any given moment" then small package sizes do increase affordability.

sectors where the BoP is integrated as customers are healthcare, consumer goods, education, and financial services. Here inclusiveness is key to sales success:

> Firms must therefore strive to infiltrate the networks and collaborate effectively with important insiders to develop a sound understanding of consumer needs. (Chikweche and Fletcher 2012)

On the other hand, the poor can also be part of value generation activities as employees of the firm, acting as distributors, or being suppliers of intermediate goods and services. Sourcing local crops from small-scale farmers is a typical example where the people at the BoP act as suppliers or employees. Establishing and training a local sales force to sell consumer products or microfinance services integrates the BoP community in the value delivery activities of the business model. In comparison to "business-as-usual," business models with an element of inclusiveness aim to undertake targeted measures to integrate the BoP and introduce innovation into their business activities. These can refer to processes as much as goods and services with the aim of making the offering more affordable and better tailored to the needs of the BoP (Simanis et al. 2008).

2. *Collaboration*

Researchers and practitioners agree that successful business ventures at the BoP are always collaborative endeavors. Therefore, building the right business ecosystem plays a vital role in every BoP business model design. A partner network can consist of customers, investors, and other stakeholders such as governmental organizations, competitors, or consultants (Sanchez and Ricart 2010). People at the BoP should not be neglected as a group of potential partners (see inclusiveness) (Hart and Sharma 2004). For example, Hindustan Unilever, located in India, developed a direct-sales program that aimed to sell Lifebuoy Soap in rural villages through partnerships with local organizations. The Shakti program trained village women as entrepreneurs and product experts who could sell the soap in their own villages (Balu 2001). Firms need to create such an ecosystem of partnerships with different stakeholders for several reasons: First, partnerships are the core source of support—either by enabling activities on the ground or by building organizational and institutional capacity. Second, they can help with the provision of knowledge about local customs and traditions or by establishing contacts with influencers in the market (Dahan et al. 2010). Third, potential sources of investment are necessary to build the business (Seelos and Mair 2007). Fourth, interaction with the local communities is crucial to develop native capabilities, which results in the ability to integrate the offering into local routines that build upon the conditions and resources faced by the BoP (Ansari et al. 2012; London and Hart 2005). Collaboration across cultures—national and business—is difficult. Firms have to learn how to manage and navigate these partnerships because, for instance, local BoP partners and non-profit organizations usually pursue different goals, practices, procedures, and values to for-profit firms (Dahan et al. 2010). Complementarities between for-profit (which possess capital, managerial, and production capabilities) and non-profit organizations (which possess expertise in specific markets, trust and legitimacy, and a good network in BoP communities) may be leveraged and can increase the potential gain for both sides (Dahan et al. 2010).

3. *Managing Complexity*

   BoP business models are usually complex as they target the double bottom line of trying to achieve a positive economic and social impact. This is accompanied by the complexity of the business model since it often deals with contradictory interdependencies (Gebauer et al. 2017). For example, a social impact brought about by firms can be neither sustained nor increased when profitability is insufficient (Polak and Warwick 2013). The need to establish partnerships with a multitude of stakeholders (see collaboration above) adds to the complexity of the BoP business model.

4. *Scalability*

   A key requirement of business models in a BoP context is to achieve sufficient scale. The literature reveals two main reasons why scalability—usually referred to as the expansion of business through the standardization of business model elements (Calton et al. 2013)—is crucial: First, it is a way to address the immensity of the need that can be found at the BoP. Second, economies of scale are necessary to achieve the financial sustainability (profitability) of the business by lowering per-unit-cost (Hammond and Kramer 2007). However, there seems to be a conflict since BoP ventures are often newly developed and highly customized endeavors that fail to reach scale and tend to remain small (Bradach 2003; Uvin et al. 2000; Whitney and Kelkar 2004). As a consequence, such models cannot be profitable enough to scale up in the long term (Hart and Christensen 2002). In fact, relatively few have successfully scaled up to meet the needs of a larger market (Bocken et al. 2016) as the attribute of scalability seems to be contradictory to the demand for tailored solutions. This is especially the case when the social impact of the double-bottom line is prioritized. Later in this book, it will be argued that multinational companies, with their regional and global factories, can achieve economies of scale by addressing the BoP and, thus reduce their per-unit-cost in production.

Expanding on the success factor of scalability, a paper by Bloom and Chatterji (2009) specifically addresses this issue and how it can be achieved in the BoP context. They developed the so-called SCALERS model based on a case study approach of the housing industry in the Mexican BoP market. Success in scaling the business model relies on seven capabilities:

(a) *Staffing* describes the necessity to acquire sufficient qualified human capital to run the endeavor. Required qualifications and capabilities mentioned to successfully work in a BoP context are cultural understanding, business-relevant knowledge, and an entrepreneurial mindset (Paddison 2014). Ansari et al. (2012) emphasize the high importance of capability development through training.

(b) *Communication* with stakeholders such as donors, employees, or other interest groups is relevant in order to inform them appropriately about the objectives and the progress of the business. This information flow is especially relevant in BoP business ventures where stakeholders are frequently donor organizations that can quickly drop their support. Stakeholders are diverse in a business model for the BoP, which raises communication and management complexity.

(c) *Alliance building* is widely accepted among researchers and practitioners as being important in order to generate shared profits. It is commonly regarded as a more successful approach than trying to accomplish goals alone. This relates to the above-mentioned success factor of collaboration.

(d) *Lobbying* is regarded as important since collaboration with governmental organizations enables organizations to obtain financial support, or favorably influences legislation. Simanis et al. (2005) highlight that the public sector and donor organizations have a part to play by providing working capital in the early stage of business ventures. However, care needs to be taken that this financial capital is not contingent upon business having to cooperate with local NGOs or addressing solely social goals, since this pushes business ideas into the area of corporate social responsibility (Paddison 2014). In addition, the government can be operatively engaged, e.g., by providing infrastructure for distribution.

(e) *Generating earnings* is a necessary scaling driver as it guarantees access to finance. Organizations may obtain revenues from sales of products or services. Alternative earning generation can come via donations, crowdsourcing platforms, grants, innovation challenge funds, or governmental grants (Bloom and Chatterji 2009; Shanmugalingam et al. 2011). This relates to the business model element of value capture.

(f) *Replication* of the business model in other settings is a key factor to scaling up (Desa and Koch 2014; Seelos and Mair 2007). Therefore, the core elements of the business models have to be standardized, whereas others should be adaptable to specific market contexts. A good example that some adaptation is required can be seen in how the first BoP business models were applied to rural Indian BoP markets. After successful implementation in Asia, practitioners tried to apply them, without modification, in Africa but failed to do so as the business environment was entirely different: Infrastructure, language, health system, cultural rites, hierarchies, history, and climate conditions are all different but, at the same time, they play an important role in business model development (Prahalad 2006).

(g) *Stimulating market forces* include engagement with the local community. The involvement of the community generates benefits in terms of social relationships that deepen and lengthen the potential impact. This includes not only the consumer but also local entrepreneurs, companies, and government organizations. Furthermore, the engagement is often regarded as a prerequisite to stimulating market forces that did not exist previously. This relates to the success factor of promotion and to the business model element of value delivery.

Many of the success factors mentioned in this chapter are either only possible with, or at least facilitated by, some level of localization on the part of the company, For instance, localization goes hand in hand with inclusiveness. The authors in Table 3.4 mentioned that the localizing part of the BoP business is an important success factor. The reason is that the required understanding of BoP customer needs, their living conditions, their culture is only possible with deep insight that cannot be gained from afar. Further, coordinating a complex partner network (collaboration) that involves BoP communities (inclusiveness) for training and last mile distribution requires a presence on the spot. Thus localization becomes a success factor in its own right and needs to feature in any BoP business model.

In summary, a variety of case studies has identified what key challenges firms face in BoP markets and provide insights into what factors need to be considered in order to create the right business model for the BoP environment. These factors are offering the right product, collaboration, a focus on inclusiveness, and local integration into the BoP ecosystem. Arguably the most important success factor from a for-profit perspective is the ability to scale the business model, which is a key lever to create affordability for BoP consumers. In general, organizations need to consider that the business model should not only be adapted to the specific context but should also be designed in ways that make it difficult to imitate so as not to lose the competitive advantage (Teece 2010). Prahalad and Hart (2002) argue that knowledge and practices to successfully address the BoP need to be rooted in local conditions and then combined with international "best practices" along entire value chains, something that can be provided by multinational companies. Therefore, it is a symbiosis of local and global knowledge and skills that result in a sustainable business model for the BoP.

3.4 Challenges Addressing Bottom of the Pyramid Markets

Addressing the BoP market segment brings with it some challenges. After having discussed the success factors, we now turn to the challenges discussed in the literature and link them to the success factors from Sect. 3.3.

First and foremost, BoP consumers in geographically fragmented markets have long been considered physically and economically inaccessible because of poor infrastructure and inadequate transportation facilities. Moreover, implementing a working distribution system is costly and therefore unattractive for companies (Tarafdar et al. 2011):

> The costs of serving the markets at the Bottom of the Pyramid can be very high. (Karnani 2007)

Therefore, improving distribution systems to reach rural areas is crucial in order to facilitate the flow of products (Chakrabarti 2011; Gold et al. 2013; Prahalad and Hart 2000). This distribution challenge has a negative impact on the success factor of ensuring availability and accessibility of the offering. Distribution becomes difficult in terms of reliability but also in terms of distribution cost. Higher costs in turn reduce affordability. Help to tackle this challenge comes from the success factor collaboration and engaging with the BoP ecosystem. This allows for cheaper and out-of-the-box approaches to distribution by collaborating with partners such as NGOs, governments, or the BoP community itself.

Secondly, BoP markets often lack access to information due to low levels of education, poor media infrastructure, and high levels of dependence on local communities (Viswanathan et al. 2008). Consequently, an exchange of information between BoP consumers and producers about the availability, usability, and ways of promoting interest in the goods and services offered is limited and hampers market activities (Schuster and Holtbrügge 2012). This poses challenges in creating awareness and generating acceptability, thus restricting market development for the products at the BoP. In order to address this, communication from within the BoP community and promotion via word-of-mouth are important. Unconventional approaches need to be developed to educate consumers with regard to the company's offering and its use.

Thirdly, the private sector often lacks relevant information on BoP consumers, for instance on their buying behavior, that is required to be able to assess market opportunities and draw up strong value propositions. Only with a sufficient understanding of customers' situation and needs is the design of a suitable offering and value proposition possible (Karamchandani et al. 2011). An adaptation of the portfolio can refer to technologies, products, and packaging that need to be aligned with the conditions at the BoP. Especially in the case of MNCs, there is a shortage of market and customer intimacy caused by their position as "outsiders" and their lack of social embeddedness (Sinkovics et al. 2014). Thus, to gain the profound knowledge required multinational companies need to engage actively with local communities.

Fourthly, there is uncertainty about consumers' cash flow and thus the reliability of payments (Karamchandani et al. 2011). This is the result of one of the key properties of BoP customers, namely their low purchasing power. Thus, authors encourage MNCs to help people at the BoP to elevate themselves above the "desperation line" of underemployment. For this to occur two interventions are crucial: (1) Help customers to increase their earnings potential and raise their purchasing power (Prahalad and Hammond 2004). (2) Help BoP customers with access to credit (e.g., microfinance) (Pitta et al. 2008). The first intervention can, for instance, be facilitated by an element of inclusiveness in the value generation activities.

Fifthly, BoP communities are often strongly influenced by sociocultural factors such as religion and traditions (Sheth 2011). To put this into perspective, Mbanya et al. (2010) describe the influence on the healthcare sector of local (health-related) beliefs and traditions in Africa. The researchers found that, owing to culturally embedded misconceptions, many people at the BoP in Africa fail to take appropriate measures for health provision and control. For instance, obesity, a diabetes risk factor, is still considered a sign of wealth, respect, and influence (Mbanya et al. 2010). The complexity of this influence is not to be underestimated since BoP communities are scattered across Africa, Asia, and Latin America, where each country or region has its own cultural traits and traditions (Kuo et al. 2016). Companies can best deal with this by localizing their activities.

Lastly, the conflict between, on the one hand, localization which comes with inclusiveness and, on the other, the need for scalability of the business model has to be resolved if a BoP business model is to be economically viable. This is problematic, since inclusiveness normally requires local involvement with the BoP community which, by definition, cannot be scaled geographically to other BoP ecosystems. Therefore, when drawing up a business model for the BoP, companies need to differentiate between business activities that can be scaled and those that are particular to each BoP community.

In conclusion, bringing products and services to BoP markets is challenging. Practitioners may face difficulties in critically assessing which criteria are most relevant for their own business. This prioritization process is further complicated by the fact that there are certain levels of interdependencies among the criteria. For instance, offering financial services impacts on the price of the service and—as a second example—the type and size of product packaging clearly influences distribution (cost) (Schuster and Holtbrügge 2012). A distribution and pricing model that is perfectly adapted to the BoP is sometimes difficult to achieve at the same time, even though both are important. Without a doubt, doing business at the BoP implies developing and creating a market instead of addressing an existing one. This creates specific challenges that need to be addressed in a business model for the BoP market.

3.5 Conclusion

Companies that use business models designed to serve developed markets in BoP markets quickly realize that the results are unsatisfactory as the BoP consumer and business environment are entirely different to developed markets (Jun et al. 2013). This led researchers and practitioners to explore the challenges and constraints that shape and characterize the BoP market (Anderson 2006). The literature on the characteristics of BoP consumers reads as follows: They have a low-income level and a limited variety of products available for which they tend to pay higher prices as a consequence of being restricted to local, informal markets. Access to formal commercial markets is restricted because of a lack of information (although with the spread of ICT technologies this is improving), a lack of education, and poor infrastructure reducing physical accessibility. BoP customers are usually located in (fragmented) rural regions or in urban slum areas. In many cases, partially due to low education levels, they adhere to traditional beliefs, e.g., concerning traditional health practices. In addition, it should be mentioned that BoP markets cannot be considered to be "ready-made." Instead, firms that want to make a profit need to create a market with a certain "trial and error" attitude (Demil and Lecocq 2010; Simanis 2011).

In order to be successful, the business models need to address the constraints linked to the consumer characteristics and the business environment at the BoP (Ausrød et al. 2017). The analysis in this chapter has identified success factors that can help to profitably address this segment despite the challenges that exist. In general, managers should carefully evaluate the voids they will confront when starting a business in BoP markets. Firms should find ways to ensure that their business models are scalable, inclusive, and collaborative (Ausrød et al. 2017; Gebauer et al. 2017; Hart and Sharma 2004; London and Hart 2005).

In detail, the identified key success factors to be incorporated into a business model for the BoP market are: A suitable product that is geared toward the (special) needs of the BoP customers, thus, a strong value proposition. This goes hand in hand with affordable pricing that considers their low purchasing power. The scalability of business models is, in many industries, a lever to reduce per-unit cost and thus make the product more affordable to BoP customers from the point of view of value creation. Another commonly mentioned point is access to the BoP customers and the distribution of products (availability). Engaging with the BoP community in the sense of inclusiveness and collaboration with BoP stakeholders can help, among other things, to set up a cost-efficient distribution to the customer, especially with regard to the so-called last-mile distribution. This makes the product available and adds affordability from the value delivery side. Inclusiveness is required to understand the needs (and pains/constraints) of the BoP population as an important input to create a strong value proposition, a suitable offering, and to build a strong network for collaboration. For this to realistically materialize, a degree of presence on the spot is required (localization). Being engaged in the BoP ecosystem helps to create awareness and to enhance the acceptability of the product with consumers. A key challenge is to convert the BoP *population* segment into a BoP *market*.

References

Amit R, Zott C (2001) Value creation in e-business. Strat Manag J 22:493–520

Amit R, Zott C (2012) Creating value through business model innovation. MIT Sloan Manag Rev 53:41–49

Anderson J (2006) A structured approach for bringing mobile telecommunications to the world's poor. Electron J Inf Syst Dev Countries 27:1–9

Anderson J, Markides C (2007) Strategic innovation at the base of the pyramid. MIT Sloan Manag Rev 49:83–88

Ansari S, Munir K, Gregg T (2012) Impact at the 'bottom of the pyramid': the role of social capital in capability development and community empowerment. J Manag Stud 49:813–842

Arnold MG (2018) Inclusive value creation for sustainability of frugal innovations in the base of the pyramid low-income contexts. J Contemp Manag 15:218–244

Ausrød VL, Sinha V, Widding Ø (2017) Business model design at the base of the pyramid. J Clean Prod 162:982–996

Balu R (2001) Strategic innovation: Hindustan Lever Ltd. Fast company on 31.5.2001. https://www.fastcompany.com/43028/strategic-innovation-hindustan-lever-ltd. Accessed 28 Aug 2018

Battistella C, de Toni AF, de Zan G, Pessot E (2017) Cultivating business model agility through focused capabilities: a multiple case study. J Bus Res 73:65–82

Bendul JC, Rosca E, Pivovarova D (2017) Sustainable supply chain models for base of the pyramid. J Clean Prod 162:107–120

Bloom PN, Chatterji AK (2009) Scaling social entrepreneurial impact. Calif Manag Rev 51:114–133

Bocken NMP, Short SW, Rana P, Evans S (2014) A literature and practice review to develop sustainable business model archetypes. J Clean Prod 65:42–56

Bocken NMP, Fil A, Prabhu J (2016) Scaling up social businesses in developing markets. J Clean Prod 139:295–308. https://doi.org/10.1016/j.jclepro.2016.08.045. Accessed 29 Aug 2019

Boons F, Lüdeke-Freund F (2013) Business models for sustainable innovation: state-of-the-art and steps towards a research agenda. J Clean Prod 45:9–19

Bowien MB (2015) The dynamics of business model transformation: innovation and internationalization. Doctoral Dissertation, ESEADE Business School, Barcelona

Bradach JL (2003) Going to scale: the challenge of replicating social programs. Stanf Soc Innov Rev 1:19–25

Breitenmoser PK (2015) Practices to initiate business model innovation in incumbent enterprises. Dissertation, Eidgenössische Technische Hochschule ETH Zürich, Nr. 22850

Budinich V, Manno Reott K, Schmidt S (2007) Hybrid value chains: social innovations and the development of the small farmer irrigation market in Mexico. Ashoka Innovators for the Public. https://papers.ssrn.com/sol3/papers.cfm?abstract_id=981223. Accessed 9 July 2020

Buliga O, Scheiner CW, Voigt K-I (2015) Business model innovation and organizational resilience: towards an integrated conceptual framework. J Bus Econ:1–24

Calton JM, Werhane PH, Hartman LP, Bevan D (2013) Building partnerships to create social and economic value at the base of the global development pyramid. J Bus Ethics 117:721–733

Casadesus-Masanell R, Ricart JE (2010) From strategy to business models and onto tactics. Long Range Plan 43:195–215

Casadesus-Masanell R, Zhu F (2013) Business model innovation and competitive imitation: the case of sponsor-based business models. Strateg Manag J 34:464–482

Castillo LG, Diehl JC, Brezet JC (2012) Design considerations for base of the pyramid (BoP) projects. Proceedings of the northern world mandate. https://www.researchgate.net/publication/257927083. Accessed 12 Nov 2019

Chakrabarti A (ed) (2011) Design for the base of the Pyramid: issues and solutions: Supporting sustainable product development. Indian Institute of Science. Research Publishing Services, Bangalore

Chan Kim W, Mauborgne R (2005) Value innovation: a leap into the blue ocean. J Bus Strateg 26:22–28

Chesbrough H (2010) Business model innovation: opportunities and Barriers. Bus Models 43:354–363

Chesbrough H, Rosenbloom RS (2002) The role of the business model in capturing value from innovation: evidence from Xerox Corporation's technology spin-off companies. Ind Corp Chang 11:529–555

Chesbrough H, Ahern S, Finn M, Guerraz S (2006) Business models for technology in the developing world: the role of non-governmental organizations. Calif Manag Rev 48:48–61

Chikweche T, Fletcher R (2011) Franchising at the bottom of the pyramid (BOP): an alternative distribution approach. Int Rev Retail Distrib Consum Res 21:343–360

Chikweche T, Fletcher R (2012) Revisiting the marketing mix at the bottom of pyramid (BOP): from theoretical considerations to practical realities. J Consum Mark 29:507–520

Chu M (2007) Commercial returns at the base of the pyramid. Innov Technol Govern Global 2:115–146

Clauss T (2016) Measuring business model innovation: conceptualization, scale development, and proof of performance. R&D Manag 47:1–19

Dahan N, Doh J, Oetzel J, Yaziji M (2010) Corporate-NGO collaboration: co-creating new business models for developing markets. Long Range Plan 43:326–342

Demil B, Lecocq X (2010) Business model evolution: in search of dynamic consistency. Long Range Plan 43:227–246

Desa G, Koch JL (2014) Scaling social impact: building sustainable social ventures at the base-of-the-pyramid. J Social Entrepren 5:146–174

Dodgson M, Gann D, Phillips N (2014) The Oxford handbook of innovation management. Oxford University Press, New York

Dubosson-Torbay M, Osterwalder A, Pigneur Y (2002) E-business model design, classification, and measurements. Thunderbird Int Bus Rev 44:5–23
Foss NJ, Saebi T (2014) Business model innovation: The organizational dimension. In: SMG Working Paper No. 2. Copenhagen Business School, Copenhagen
Gassmann O, Frankenberger K, Csik M (2013) Geschäftsmodelle entwickeln: 55 innovative Konzepte mit dem St. Galler Business Model Navigator. Carl Hanser Verlag GmbH Co KG
Gebauer H, Haldimann M, Saul CJ (2017) Business model innovations for overcoming barriers in the base-of-the-pyramid market. Ind Innov 24:543–568
Giesen E, Berman SJ, Bell R, Blitz A (2007) Three ways to successfully innovate your business model. Strateg Leadersh 35:27–33
Giesen E, Riddleberger E, Christner R, Bell R (2010) When and how to innovate your business model. Strateg Leadersh 38:17–26
GIZ (2012) Bringing medicines to low-income markets. A guide to creating inclusive business models for pharmaceutical companies. Eschborn.
Goethals FG (2011) Mindfully innovating your business model. Gestion 2000(28):47–61
Gold S, Hahn R, Seuring S (2013) Sustainable supply chain management in "Base of the Pyramid" food projects—A path to triple bottom line approaches for multinationals? Int Bus Rev 22:784–799
Goyal S, Sergi BS, Kapoor A (2014) Understanding the key characteristics of an embedded business model for the base of the pyramid markets. Econ Soc 7:26–40
Gradl C, Knobloch C (2010) Inclusive business guide. How to develop business and fight poverty. Endeva UG, Berlin
Gummesson E, Nenonen S, Storbacka K (2010) Business model design: conceptualizing networked value co-creation. Int J Qual Serv Sci 2:43–59
Habib M, Zurawicki L (2010) The bottom of the pyramid: key roles for businesses. J Bus Econ Res 8:23–32
Hamel G (2001) Leading the revolution Interview with Gary Hamel. Strateg Leadersh 29:4–10
Hammond AL, Kramer W (2007) The next 4 Billion: market size and business strategy at the base of the pyramid. World Resources Institute, Washington, DC
Hammond AL, Kramer WJ, Katz RS, Tran JT, Walker C (2007) The next 4 billion. Innov Technol Govern Global 2:147–158
Hart SL, Christensen CM (2002) The great leap: driving innovation from the base of the pyramid. MIT Sloan Manag Rev 44:51
Hart SL, Milstein MB (2003) Creating sustainable value. Acad Manag Perspect 17:56–67
Hart SL, Sharma S (2004) Engaging fringe stakeholders for competitive imagination. Acad Manag Perspect 18:7–18
IBM Global Business Services (2006) Expanding the Innovation Horizon 2006. CEO Study – Executive Summary. IBM Corporation, New York. http://www.businessmodelinnovation.org.sg/wp-content/uploads/2015/01/global_ceo_study.pdf. Accessed 19 Jan 2020
Johnson MW, Christensen CM, Kagermann H (2008) Reinventing your business model. Harv Bus Rev 86:50–59
Jose PD (2008) Rethinking the BOP: new models for the new millennium-Academic perspective. IIMB Manag Rev 20:198ff
Jun S, Lee D, Park J (2013) Determining business models in bottom-of-the-pyramid markets. Ind Manag Data Syst 113:1064–1082
Karamchandani A, Kubzansky M, Lalwani N (2011) Is the bottom of the pyramid really for you. Harv Bus Rev 89:107–111
Karnani A (2007) The mirage of marketing to the bottom of the pyramid: how the private sector can help alleviate poverty. Calif Manag Rev 49:90–111
Khanna T, Palepu K (1997) Why focused strategies may be wrong for emerging markets. Harv Bus Rev 75:41–43
Kuo T, Hanafi J, Sun W, Robielos R (2016) The effects of national cultural traits on BOP consumer behavior. Sustainability 8:272ff

Kuriyan R, Ray I, Kammen D (2008) How to use technology to spur development. Issues Sci Technol 24:70–74

London T (2007) A base-of-the-pyramid perspective on poverty alleviation. University of Michigan

London T, Hart SL (2004) Reinventing strategies for emerging markets: beyond the transnational model. J Int Bus Stud 35:350–370

London T, Hart SL (2005) Developing native capability. Stanf Soc Innov Rev 3:28–33

London T, Anupindi R, Sheth S (2010) Creating mutual value: lessons learned from ventures serving base of the pyramid producers. J Bus Res 63:582–594

Magretta J (2002) Why business models matter. Harv Bus Rev 80:86–92

Mahadevan B (2000) Business models for Internet-based e-commerce: an anatomy. Calif Manag Rev 42:55–69

Mason K, Chakrabarti R (2017) The role of proximity in business model design: making business models work for those at the bottom of the pyramid. Ind Mark Manag 61:67–80

Matsumoto K (2018) Critical factors for success among social enterprises in India. JICA-RI Working Paper, pp 1–61

Mbanya JCN, Motala AA, Sobngwi E, Assah FK, Enoru ST (2010) Diabetes in sub-Saharan Africa. Lancet 375:2254–2266

Miles RE, Miles G, Snow CC (2006) Collaborative entrepreneurship: a business model for continuous innovation. Organ Dyn 35:1–11

Mitchell D, Coles C (2003) The ultimate competitive advantage of continuing business model innovation. J Bus Strateg 24:15–21

Morris M, Schindehutte M, Allen J (2005) The entrepreneur's business model: toward a unified perspective. J Bus Res 58:726–735

Oodith PD, Parumasur SB (2013) Tapping into the bottom of the pyramid (BOP) market in South Africa: possible and how? Corp Ownersh Control 11:280–294

Osterwalder A, Pigneur Y (2010) Business model generation: a handbook for visionaries, game changers, and challengers. Wiley

Osterwalder A, Pigneur Y, Tucci CL (2005a) Clarifying business models: origins, present and future of the concept. Commun Assoc Inf Syst 16:1–25

Osterwalder A, Pigneur Y, Tucci CL (2005b) Clarifying business models: origins, present, and future of the concept. Commun Assoc Inf Syst 16:1ff

Osterwalder A, Pigneur Y, Clark T (2010) Business model generation: a handbook for visionaries, game changers, and challengers. Wiley, Hoboken, NJ

Paddison L (2014) 10 lessons for doing business with base of the pyramid markets. https://www.theguardian.com/sustainable-business/10-lessons-doing-business-base-of-the-pyramid-markets. Accessed 18 Aug 2018

Parmigiani A, Rivera-Santos M (2015) Sourcing for the base of the pyramid: constructing supply chains to address voids in subsistence markets. J Oper Manag 33:60–70

Pitta DA, Guesalaga R, Marshall P (2008) The quest for the fortune at the bottom of the pyramid: potential and challenges. J Consum Mark 25:393–401

Polak P, Warwick M (2013) The business solution to poverty: designing products and services for three billion new customers. Berrett-Koehler, San Francisco

Prahalad CK (2006) The fortune at the bottom of the pyramid: eradicating poverty through profits. Wharton School Publishing, Upper Saddle River, NJ

Prahalad CK, Hammond AL (2004) Selling to the poor. Foreign Policy 142:30–37

Prahalad CK, Hart SL (2000) Raising the bottom of the pyramid: strategies for sustainable growth. https://www.academia.edu/. Accessed 17 Aug 2018

Prahalad CK, Hart SL (2002) The fortune at the bottom of the pyramid. Strat Bus 26:2–14

Raj K, Aithal PS (2018) The concept of cockroach theory of sustainable and scalable organizational and Individual growth. International Journal of Advanced Trends in Engineering and Technology 3:146–149

Ricart JE, Enright MJ, Ghemawat P, Hart SL, Khanna T (2004) New frontiers in international strategy. J Int Bus Stud 35:175–200

Sanchez P, Ricart JE (2010) Business model innovation and sources of value creation in low-income markets. Eur Manag Rev 7:138–154
Sánchez CM, Schmid AS (2013) Base of the pyramid success: a relational view. South Asian J Glob Bus Res 2:59–81
Schallmo DRA (2013) Geschäftsmodelle erfolgreich entwickeln und implementieren: Mit Aufgaben und Kontrolfragen. Springer, Berlin
Schallmo D, Moser M, Brecht L (2012) Geschäftsmodelle in Emerging Markets-Herausforderungen, Kompatibilität, Best practices. Market Rev St Gallen 29:52–60
Schuster T, Holtbrügge D (2012) Market entry of multinational companies in markets at the bottom of the pyramid: a learning perspective. Int Bus Rev 21:817–830
Schuster T, Holtbrügge D (2014) Resource dependency, innovative strategies, and firm performance in BOP markets. J Prod Innov Manag 31:43–59
Seelos C, Mair J (2007) Profitable business models and market creation in the context of deep poverty: a strategic view. Acad Manag Perspect 21:49–63
Seelos C (2010a) Theorizing and strategizing with models: Generative models of business models. In: IESE business school working paper no. 857. IESE Business School–University of Navarra, Barcelona
Shanmugalingam C, Graham J, Tucker S, Mulgan G (2011) Growing social ventures. The role of intermediaries and investors, who they are, what they do, and what they become. Nesta, London
Sheth JN (2011) Impact of emerging markets on marketing: rethinking existing perspectives and practices. J Mark 75:166–182
Shukla S, Bairiganjan S (2011) The base of pyramid distribution challenge. Centre for Development Finance, Chennai
Simanis E (2011) Needs, needs, everywhere, but not a BoP market to tap. In: London T, Hart S (eds) Next generation business strategies for the base of the pyramid. Financial Times Press, Upper Saddle River, NJ, pp 103–126
Simanis E (2012) Reality check at the bottom of the pyramid. Harv Bus Rev 90:120–125
Simanis E, Duke D (2014) Profits at the bottom of the pyramid. Harv Bus Rev 92:86–93
Simanis E, Hart S, Enk G, Duke D, Gordon M, Lippert A (2005) Strategic initiatives at the base of the pyramid. A protocol for mutual value creation. In: Base of the Pyramid Protocol Workshop Group, Wingspread Conference Center. Racine
Simanis E, Hart S, Duke D (2008) The base of the pyramid protocol: beyond "basic needs" business strategies. Innov Technol Govern Global 3:57–84
Sinkovics N, Sinkovics RR, Yamin M (2014) The role of social value creation in business model formulation at the bottom of the pyramid – implications for MNEs? Int Bus Rev 23:692–707
Stewart DW, Zhao Q (2000) Internet marketing, business models, and public policy. J Public Policy Mark 19:287–296
Tarafdar M, Anekal P, Singh R (2011) Market development at the bottom of the pyramid: examining the role of information and communication technologies. Inf Technol Dev 18:311–331
Teece DJ (2010) Business models, business strategy and innovation. Bus Models 43:172–194
Timmers P (1998) Business models for electronic markets. Electron Markets 8:3–8
UNDP (2013) Realizing Africa's wealth: building inclusive business for shared prosperity. A UNDP African Facility for Inclusive Markets Report. New York
UNDP (2014) Private sector success stories from UNDP country offices in Africa. Addis Abeba
Uvin P, Jain PS, Brown LD (2000) Think large and act small: toward a new paradigm for NGO scaling up. World Dev 28:1409–1419
Verstraete T, Jouison E (2007) Three theories to frame the concept of business model in context of firm foundation
Viswanathan M, Gajendiran S, Venkatesan R (2008) Enabling consumer and entrepreneurial literacy in subsistence marketplaces. Springer, Dordrecht
Whitney P, Kelkar A (2004) Designing for the base of the pyramid. Des Manag Rev 15:41–47
Yip GS (2004) Using strategy to change your business model. Bus Strateg Rev 15:17–24

Yunus M, Moingeon B, Lehmann-Ortega L (2010) Building social business models: lessons from the Grameen experience. Bus Models 43:308–325

Zott C, Amit R (2008) The fit between product market strategy and business model: implications for firm performance. Strateg Manag J 29:1–26

Zott C, Amit R (2010) Designing your future business model: an activity system perspective. Long Range Plan 43:216–226

Zott C, Amit R, Massa L (2011) The business model: recent developments and future research. J Manag 37:1019–1042

Zott C, Amit R (2013) The business model: A theoretically anchored robust construct for strategic analysis. Strateg Organ 11:403–411

Chapter 4
Political and Macroeconomic Situation in Sub-Saharan Africa

Africa consists of 54[1] very heterogeneous countries from a geographic, ethnographic, economic, religious, and political point of view. Of these, 48 countries are in Sub-Saharan Africa. The countries differ in many ways:

- Sixteen of the countries are landlocked.
- Their populations ranged from 97,000 (Seychelles) to 195 million (Nigeria) in 2018.
- GDP (real, 2010) was between USD274 million (Sao Tomé) and 469 bn (Nigeria) in 2018.
- The Human Development Index score of 2019 varied between 0.377 (Niger) and 0.728 (Botswana; roughly the same as China).
- The share of rural population ranged from 11% (Gabon) to 87% (Burundi) in 2018.
- Whereas Eswatini (formerly Swaziland) had a solid manufacturing sector with a 29% share of GDP in 2018, this share was only 2% in Liberia; most SSA countries have a single-digit share of manufacturing in their GDP.
- The share of service industries in GDP in Sao Tome and Principe was 71.8% while, at the low end, it was a mere 28.8% in Togo in 2018 (World Bank n.d.-d; UNCTAD n.d.-b; UNDP n.d.).

For companies, this heterogeneity means that there is no "one solution fits all" business approach for SSA countries. Some similarities are found regardless of all differences. On the downside, with the exception of very few countries (Mauretania, Seychelles, Mauritius), poverty is well above global levels (measured as percentage of population living on less than USD 1.9, 2011 PPP basis). Poverty levels can reach beyond 60% of the population in extreme cases (Burundi, Madagascar, Rwanda)

[1]Western Sahara is not considered as a separate country as it remains a disputed territory.

P. von Carlowitz, *Success in the Bottom of the Pyramid Market in Africa*,
SpringerBriefs in Business, https://doi.org/10.1007/978-3-030-59068-0_4

(World Bank n.d.-d).[2] The Doing Business Conditions 2019 as measured by the World Bank are amongst the worst in the world (World Bank 2020). On the upside, Sub-Saharan Africa is the most dynamic region worldwide. The population will double by 2050 and real economic growth of 6.8% p.a. over the period 2000–2017 was observed, which is slightly more than Asia's average growth. SSA has the second-fastest urbanization growth rate in the world with an increase in the urban population of 4.1% p.a. between 2010 and 2018, while the world growth figure stood at half that. Some countries had annual urbanization growth rates of over 6% (Uganda, Equatorial Guinea) and key countries like Nigeria and Ethiopia have growth rates of 4.8% p.a. (World Bank n.d.-d). Africa's improvement in the Human Development Index with a rate of 1.03% p.a. from 2010 to 2018 is the second fastest improvement rate worldwide after Asia (1.18% p.a.) (UNDP 2019).

The following section provides an overview of the political, macroeconomic, and social situation. This is followed by a section on the most relevant conditions for doing business in SSA countries and some insights on the Bottom of the Pyrami in Sub-Saharan Africa. The aim is to set the stage for the analysis of the healthcare system and the pharmaceutical industry.

4.1 Political and Social Overview and Outlook for Sub-Saharan Africa

Africa remains the most vulnerable continent in the world despite various improvements in political stability indices and conflict indicators. Looking at the medium- and long-term political risk indicators, 34 out of 48 SSA countries have an index value of 6 or 7 (7 being the highest risk) in 2020 (Credendo 2020). Adding the COFACE country medium- and long-term risk rating, 16 countries show the two highest-risk ratings of D or E (Coface 2020). However, these ratings, albeit always at the lower end, have tended to fluctuate in many countries over the years as many SSA countries are in a phase of political transformation. Looking back at the super election year of 2015, none of the 16 presidential or parliamentary elections ended in significant violence even when the opposition candidate won (Afrika Verein der Deutschen Wirtschaft e.V. 2015).

Since elections are phases of potential political and/or social unrest, Table 4.1 provides an overview of planned upcoming presidential elections in key markets.

It remains to be seen how these elections will turn out. Will there be political turmoil or social unrest or will relative stability prevail? From the past, a trend toward stability can be seen:

> Subsaharan Africa's tendency for political instability has declined. (Bello-Schünemann and Moyer 2018: 2)

[2]Note that the data availability is sketchy and the numbers are not necessarily for the same year but all from the period 2013–2016.

Table 4.1 Upcoming presidential elections in important SSA countries

Country	Election year
Côte d'Ivoire	2020
Ethiopia	2024
Ghana	2024
Kenya	2022
Nigeria	2023
Rwanda	2024
Senegal	2026
South Africa	2024
Tanzania	2020
Uganda	2021

Source: Economist Intelligence Unit (2019)

The domestic policy situation shows a declining number of public protests since 2013 but when one looks at the long-term trend since 2000 they have risen. This indicates some level of citizen discontent about government (policies). The reasons for public protest have shifted from initially political to economic discontent led by demands for higher wages and better working conditions. The former key concern of protest was against the country's political process and has sharply declined since 2011 (AfDB et al. 2017). Despite peaceful public protest being part of freedom of speech, which cannot be considered negative, excessive protest can disrupt economic activity. Various surveys in the years 2016/2018 on the governance and performance of African public institutions show that the most pressing issues of the African population regarding public services and policy areas are unemployment (10.3%), health (9.5%), water supply (8.7%), food shortage (8.4%), poverty (7.9%), and management of the economy (7.6%). Most of these are issues directly related to survival (water, food, poverty) or indirectly related (unemployment, health). This ranking can be understood as an indication of the level of human and economic development (Afrobarometer n.d.). This assessment has economic implications as it affects labor productivity, which is key to the global competitiveness of the African countries.

Box 4.1. What the citizens think! (Afrobarometer n.d.)[3]

Three quarters of the African citizens surveyed prefer a democracy but only 44% are "satisfied" or "fairly satisfied" with their country's performance in reaching/running a democracy. At the same time, the trust that the population has in the president is significantly higher (57%) than the trust in parliament (48%). The same picture evolves when looking at the level of satisfaction with the president's performance (60%) and that of parliament (45%). The difference between the trust and the performance regarding the president is small

(continued)

[3]The Afrobarometer surveys eight SSA countries on a regular basis. They are: Benin, Côte d'Ivoire, Kenya, Malawi, Mali, Uganda, Zambia, Zimbabwe. In each country more than 1000 citizens are interviewed.

Box 4.1 (continued)
with a slight upside in terms of performance. Looking at parliament citizens tend to see a performance that is below the trust they bestow on parliament. This points to a high level of dissatisfied citizens with regard to the working of democracy in their country.

In terms of fear of political intimidation, the majority in most countries sees no or very little intimidation with two exceptions: Kenya and Zimbabwe. Although the vast majority of citizens surveyed trust their president to abide by the law, roughly 25% still think their president does not do so. By the same token, trust in the police is limited. For all countries the proportion trusting the police and not trusting them is equal; in Kenya, a stunning 60% do not tend to trust the police. Freedom of speech is limited: Only 35% see freedom of speech guaranteed in their country, which is roughly the same share that does not see it guaranteed at all. The least freedom of speech exists in Zimbabwe and Côte d'Ivoire, both with a low 20%; the highest freedom of speech level is found in Kenya, Malawi, and Uganda, all above 40%.

Looking at the perception of African citizens regarding corruption they find government and business corruption equally rampant with more than 40% of respondents stating that "all of them" or "most of them" are corrupt. If you add "some of them" then the figure rises to more than 80%. At the same time, the citizens do not see their governments as being capable of dealing with corruption (nearly 70% state that it is "very" or "fairly bad"). Only in Benin do 44% of citizens see their government acting against corruption.

In general, the population is discontent with the provision of public services except for four countries (Cabo Verde, Ethiopia, Senegal, and Rwanda) which score above 3.5 out of 7. All other countries are low performers. This negatively impacts consumers and companies that require public services, for instance, in administration and infrastructure (AfDB et al. 2017). The African Integrity Indicators 2018 support this assessment: Despite regulations for various governance aspects, practical implementation frequently shows significant weaknesses. This results in the negative perception of many countries' citizens when it comes to their assessment of public services and governance. For instance, on average, the independence of the judicial system is guaranteed by law (score of 55.5) but in practice this is much less so (score 39.8). Corruption is considered illegal in all SSA countries in legislation (score 100) but, on the implementation side, corruption investigation bodies are ineffective (score of 34.2). While legislation pushes for the investigation of public service corruption (score 53.7), it is less intensively pursued (score 33.8). This gap between law and practice also extends into areas that are directly relevant for business. Public procurement legally requires competitive tendering (score 94) which in reality is not the case (score 43.5) (Globalintegrity 2018). Thus, the result of the population survey (see Box 4.1 above) and the high-level integrity indicators draw a similar picture of various policy and implementation issues for SSA government institutions. The discrepancies described between regulation and implementation lead to trust issues in the population and for companies it holds risks they need to manage.

One of the urgent political concerns is reducing poverty as the Afrobarometer surveys 2016/2018 show. Poverty is important as it can be a source of social unrest and instability. It remains high in SSA despite continuous relative improvements and discussion about a rising middle class. According to the World Bank, the share of population living below USD 1.90 (2011 PPP) per day in SSA has dropped by 13 percentage points since 2002 to a level of 42.3% in 2015. For the second poverty threshold at USD 3.20 (2011 PPP) per day, the figure for SSA is 68% of the population, down by 9.5 percentage points since 2002. Despite the substantial decline in the proportion of poor people in the total population the performance compared to the rest of the world is limited: On a global level, the respective shares declined by 15.5 percentage points and nearly 21 percentage points, respectively (World Bank n.d.-d). The main cause of poverty remains high unemployment, especially among the youth. Estimates from the African Development Bank show that half of African youth are either unemployed or inactive in the labor market, with an additional 35% in vulnerable employment. In addition, SSA has one of the highest Gini coefficients of all world regions with 0.43, indicating unequal income distribution (AfDB et al. 2017). Looking at individual SSA countries, many of the countries have high inequality of income distribution. South Africa, Namibia, and Botswana are the least equal income distributed countries on the continent (and worldwide) with Gini coefficients going beyond 0.6 (World Bank n.d.-d).[4]

Urbanization in SSA is progressing fast and so are slums. The share of urban population has been rising since the year 2000 when the share of the urban population stood at 31% compared to a share of 38% today, which is the lowest urbanization rate worldwide but the second-highest urbanization growth rate with 1.4% p.a.[5] By 2030 it is expected that 50%, and by 2050 more than 60%, of SSA's population will be living in urban areas (UN 2019). East Africa currently has the lowest urbanization rate with 25% of the population, while the other regions stand at about 45% and Southern Africa at 62%. This fast urbanization rate creates large pressure on urban infrastructure and usually results in growing slum populations with high poverty rates since urban areas cannot absorb the high influx of people. The share of the urban population that lives in slums declined from 65% to 56% of the urban population between 2000 and 2014. Despite these declining shares, the absolute figure has increased from 128 million people to 200 million in the same period. The share of the slum population in the urban population in 2014 varied from 23% in South Africa to 93% in South Sudan (UN-HABITAT 2016). Hence, when searching for the Bottom of the Pyramid segment it is also found in the urban areas as more than half of the poor population in SSA lives in cities.

To sum up, political instability remains high despite distinct improvements. Of more concern is the population's discontent with the performance of government institutions in many countries, a situation that can potentially lead to social unrest.

---

[4]For comparison: the USA (0.41) and Germany (0.32).

[5]This value is the CAGR of the change of the urbanization *rate*. The 4.1% p.a. mentioned earlier relates to the *urban* population.

The danger of potential social unrest is related to the high rate of poor people, especially clustered in the slums of the urban areas. The higher risks of social and political instability, compared with more developed regions in the world, imply greater business risk, harsher business conditions, and higher costs. This affects not only *whether* companies address the market but also *how* they need to address it.

4.2 Economic Situation and Outlook for Sub-Saharan Africa[6]

Sub-Saharan Africa boasted impressive growth between 2000 and 2018 by more than doubling real GDP in that period, roughly the same as Asia. Europe only managed to grow, cumulatively, by 30% and North America by some 40%. Due to the fast population growth, the well-being of the population, crudely measured by GDP per capita is not keeping up. In SSA it only grew by 40% (GDP by 130%) while in Europe it rose by 23%, which is close to overall economic growth. The top performers of the more sizeable economies in SSA in terms of GDP and GDP per capita (in brackets) are as follows: the clear leader is Ethiopia growing nearly fivefold (GDP per capita grew threefold). Countries that trebled the size of their economy are Ghana (90%), Mozambique (doubling), Nigeria (80%), Uganda (70%), and Tanzania (90%) (UNCTAD n.d.-c). Despite the fact that high population growth can be a future economic growth driver it currently results in much lower GDP per capita growth than overall GDP expansion. Nonetheless, the overall growth of SSA makes it an increasingly interesting market from a business perspective. A survey amongst experts of 22 Austrian companies active in SSA revealed that the main motive for business activities is the current and future sales potential (Carlowitz 2019). However, people's prosperity is lagging behind so companies have to find ways to address the lower middle-income customer segment and the Bottom of the Pyramid segment.

In 2018 two countries (Nigeria and South Africa) accounted for over 50%, and the largest five economies (the former two plus Angola, Ghana, and Kenya) combined accounted for nearly two-thirds of SSA's GDP (UNCTAD n.d.-c). Of these countries, three are commodity-based with two depending on oil and gas (Nigeria and Angola) and one on minerals (South Africa). Their weak performance since 2014, when world commodity prices dropped, has subdued SSA's regional economic growth in the past years. The regional composition of the continent's growth keeps changing. Up to 2014, when oil and gas prices were high, it was especially West African countries like Nigeria that were strong regional drivers of SSA's growth. After world commodity prices declined, the growth center shifted to East

[6]The economic implications of the Covid-19 pandemic are not included in this chapter as at time of publication the pandemic was ongoing. For a first assessment see IMF (2020). For the purpose of this book the medium- and long-term outlook suffices.

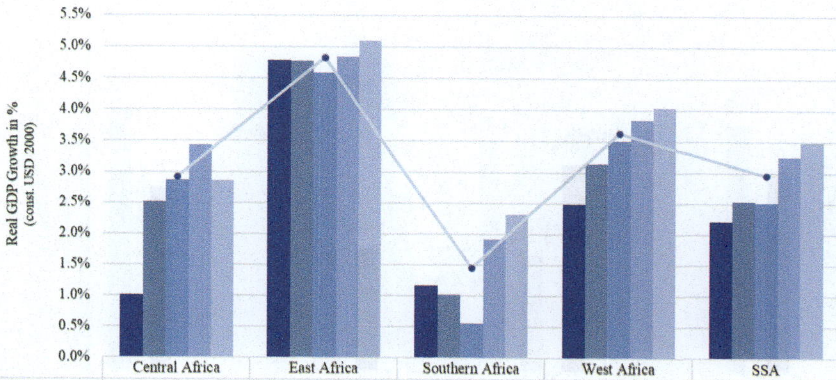

	Central Africa	East Africa	Southern Africa	West Africa	SSA
2017	1.0%	4.8%	1.2%	2.5%	2.2%
2018	2.5%	4.8%	1.0%	3.1%	2.5%
2019	2.9%	4.6%	0.6%	3.5%	2.5%
2020	3.4%	4.8%	1.9%	3.8%	3.3%
2021	2.9%	5.1%	2.3%	4.0%	3.5%
Avg. 2017-2021	2.9%	4.8%	1.5%	3.6%	3.0%

Fig. 4.1 Regional split of GDP growth 2017–2021 (excl. Covid-19 effects). (The forecasts are the pre-Covid-19 pandemic values provided by the African Development Bank.) Source: Own Illustration, based on AfDB (n.d.)

Africa. Overall, however, the SSA region is expected to grow at an average rate of 3.0% p.a. (in real terms USD 2000) between 2017 and 2021 (see Fig. 4.1) which includes forecasts for 2019–2021 (AfDB n.d., 2019). However, the current situation with the Covid-19 pandemic has made the initial forecasts for the short term obsolete. According to the International Monetary Fund, the economic growth for most countries worldwide is expected to be negative in 2020 and a rebound from 2021 is forecast. The IMF forecast, from April 2020, for Sub-Saharan Africa for 2020 stands at −1.6% with a rebound to 4.1% in 2021. South Africa and Nigeria, by far the biggest countries in SSA, have also suffered in 2020 with growth forecasts of −5.8% and −3.4% and stronger rebound values in 2021, as initially forecasted, of 4.0% and 2.4%, respectively. Despite this negative effect, some countries, mainly in East Africa (Kenya, Uganda, Tanzania, Ethiopia), are expected to continue to grow despite the pandemic. Commodity-based economies (natural resources) have been hit hard by the pandemic as demand for their main products has completely collapsed (e.g., Angola, Nigeria, Botswana, Democratic Republic of Congo) (IMF n.d.-a).

Comparing the impact of Covid-19 on the initial regional growth forecast shown in Fig. 4.1 it can be seen that Southern Africa (Southern African Development Community) is hit hardest, with −3.4% contraction in 2020 and growth of 3.9% in 2021 (mainly driven by South Africa), followed by West Africa (Economic Community of West African States) with a decline of −1.4% (2020) and a rebound of 3.9% (2021). Only East Africa (East African Community) continues to grow, albeit at a lower rate: in 2020 growth is expected to stand at 2% and in 2021 it will be back to a "normal" 5.2% (IMF n.d.-a). Despite the backlash of the extreme event of

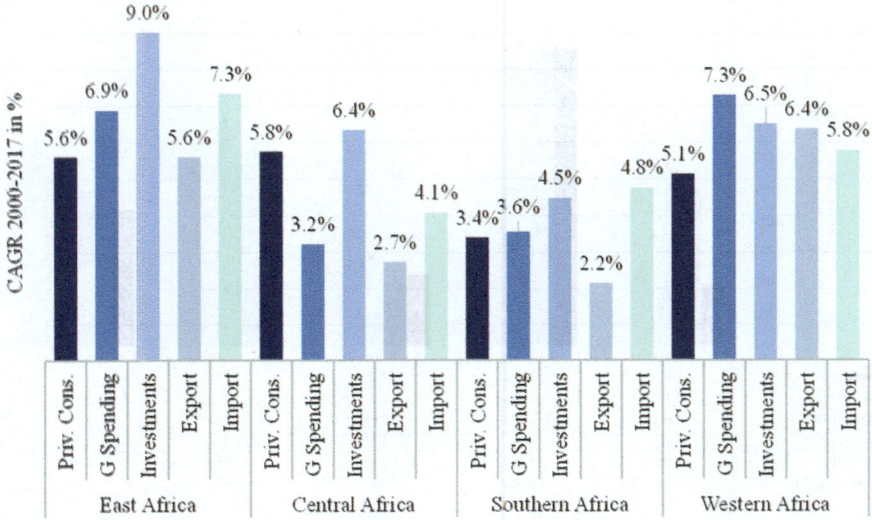

Fig. 4.2 Growth drivers of GDP by component 2000–2017 (CAGR). Source: Own Illustration, based on UNCTAD (n.d.-c), National Account Statistics

Covid-19, it is assumed that Africa will recover and continue on its initial medium-term growth path. The IMF's long-term forecast expects an average annual growth rate in real GDP of around 3.8% between 2019 and 2024. The underperforming "giants" in SSA, namely Nigeria (2.5% p.a.) and South Africa (1.5% p.a.), will continue to slow down overall SSA economic growth (IMF n.d.-b).

A significant positive correlation exists between diversification and economic growth resilience: The more diversified SSA economies have shown higher and more robust GDP growth in the past years, led by Côte d'Ivoire, Rwanda, and Ethiopia, which all grew in the range of 7–10% p.a. (AfDB et al. 2017). In addition, improvements in the quality of macroeconomic governance and business conditions (see Sect. 4.3) have strengthened the growth effects. African countries are among the top reformers in the world and approximately 25% of global reforms were undertaken in SSA economies with Togo, Nigeria, Kenya, and Zimbabwe being the leading reformer countries (World Bank 2020). General growth drivers—depending on the economy—are commodity prices for many countries, especially in Central and Western Africa, as they are the main contributors to exports and (foreign direct) investments. Turning to the growth drivers of GDP by region in more detail, some heterogeneity is observed (Fig. 4.2).

Sub-Saharan African economic growth is mainly driven by private consumption (for all regions the largest share of GDP) as a result of a growing population and a rising middle class (AfDB 2019; UNECA 2019). The second major source of growth is investment, which is largely driven by an increase in public infrastructure investment. Within investment figures, foreign direct investment (FDI) plays an important role. There are regional differences in the relevance of and reasons for investment: In

East Africa, the investment share of GDP accounted for 30% in 2017 due to the diversified structures of the economies while in Central Africa, it stood at 27% of GDP thanks to investments in the mining sector. This high share of investment in GDP and its high growth rate in East Africa indicate that investment is not necessarily linked to natural resources. Across all SSA countries, 8.5% of Gross Capital Formation was from FDI in 2017 (the figure for the world stood at 7.5%) with double-digit shares in Eastern (13.9%) and Western Africa (11.2%) showing a high dependence on foreign investment to build the economies' capacities (for comparison the share for China is 2.6% and for Germany, it is 4.9%) (UNCTAD n.d.-c).

Especially in East and West Africa, government expenditure shows high growth rates but the contribution to economic growth is limited as the public sector accounts for a limited share of GDP. For East Africa, the trade balance is significantly negative (in real and nominal terms) as the region is strongly dependent on imports for commercial agriculture and manufacturing business as well as in consumer goods to satisfy high domestic demand. The resource-rich regions of Central and Western Africa were net exporters in 2017 as commodity prices rose again (UNCTAD n.d.-c). Going forward, the current account deficit of −3.3% of GDP (2017–2024) for SSA and for nearly all SSA countries (IMF n.d.-b) shows that the countries are, and will remain, generally import-based markets.

Turning to the economies' structure by sector on a regional level the high dependence on world market prices becomes apparent. East and Western Africa are strongly dependent on agriculture, of which many of the products are world market priced. Central Africa is highly dependent on mining products (30% of total value added) (see Fig. 4.3).

Looking at the economic structure over time an economic transformation can be observed for the four SSA regions. It is visible in the percentage change of the sectors' value added in total value added (constant USD) as shown in Fig. 4.4.

It appears that SSA is embarking on a new type of economic transformation path, shifting from primary industries (agriculture, mining) to service-based industries, structurally bypassing the manufacturing sector. Looking at manufacturing the result is very differentiated with the relative share of manufacturing in East and Southern Africa falling while stagnating in the other two regions. This has economic and social implications as manufacturing industries are usually (lower skilled) employment-intensive. With regard to agriculture, the development is different. Its share is shrinking everywhere except in West Africa while that of the service sector is increasing. The most distinct shift away from agriculture is seen in East Africa. Turning to mining, the strongest shift from mining to services is observed in West Africa. This has significantly reduced the strong direct and indirect dependency of GDP on commodity prices in many African countries. Nigeria, for instance, has started on a diversification process, moving away from its strong dependency on mining to a stronger service orientation[7] with the share of oil in GDP dropping from

[7]One reason for the strong decline in mining and utilities is the drop in investment activities in the utility infrastructure sector due to a lack of government funds as a result of the low tax income caused by the drop in commodity prices.

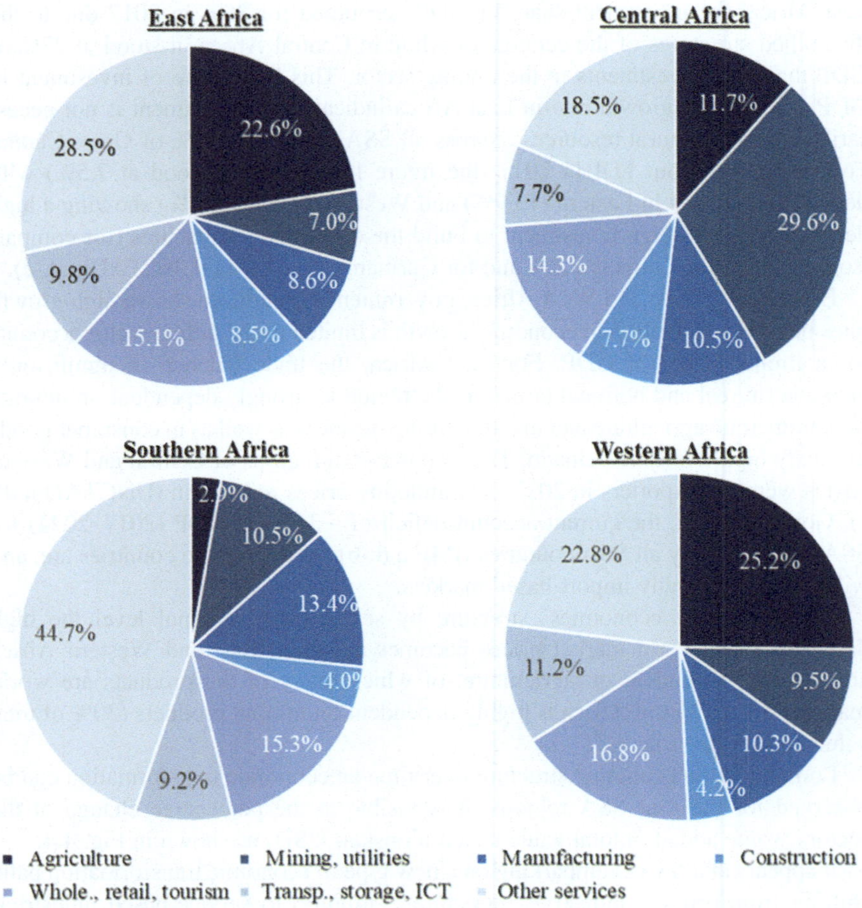

Fig. 4.3 Economic structure by SSA region 2017 (share of sector value added in GDP in %, constant USD basis). Source: Own Illustration, based on UNCTAD (n.d.-c), National Account Statistics

over 25% in 2000 to only 10% in 2016 (AfDB et al. 2017). Interestingly and contrary to common understanding, the share of mining and utilities in Western Africa is declining not only because of the weak performance of the mining sector (it grew by just over 3% p.a. between 2000 and 2017) but because of even higher growth in manufacturing and the service industries, all above 6% p.a. (UNCTAD n.d.-b). It will, however, be many years before dependency on commodities is significantly reduced, especially when indirect effects related to foreign exchange earnings and tax revenues are included: The former reduces the import potential of needed goods, and the latter limits government revenue and, ultimately, public spending.

FDI inflows facilitate this structured transformation. Looking at FDI project *numbers*, the majority of the total 718 projects is found in the service industries

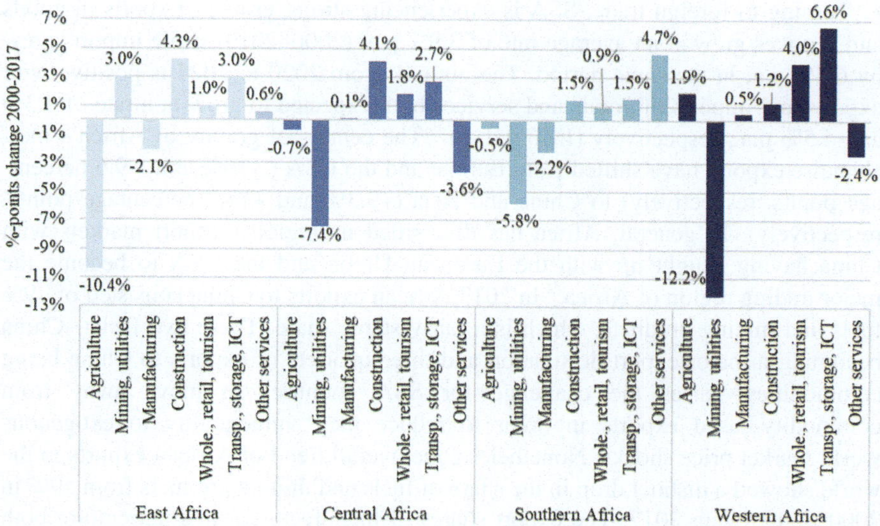

Fig. 4.4 Structural economic transformation by SSA regions 2000–2017 (percentage points difference in shares of sector value added in GDP between 2000 and 2017, constant USD). Source: Own Illustration, based on UNCTAD (n.d.-c), National Account Statistics

such as transportation (41), business services (80), software/IT services (53), financial services (67), and communication (45). Of these, all grew except financial services (−44%) and business services (−22%). Turning to FDI projects by business activities, most are related to manufacturing, sales and marketing, and business services (Analyze Africa 2017). FDI activity by *value* into Africa declined between 2012 and 2017 but recovered—against the global trend (−27%)—in 2018, growing by 11% to a total inflow of USD 46 bn. Of this USD 32 bn went to SSA. Despite SSA's low global share in FDI inflow in 2018 (2.5% of world FDI share), it plays a significant role in the economic development of Sub-Saharan African countries. FDI accounted for 1.9% of Africa's GDP in 2018 (Germany 0.67%, China 1.02% for comparison) (UNCTAD n.d.-c). On a regional level, West Africa saw a drop of 15% to USD 9.6 bn mainly due to a decline in Nigeria. East Africa stabilized at 13 bn despite an 18% drop in Ethiopia which was offset by the 27% increase in Kenya. Central Africa and Southern Africa, the latter driven by South Africa, exhibited significant growth compensating for the loss in Western Africa (UNCTAD 2019). In terms of FDI *value* into Africa, 40% of the announced FDI value went into real estate followed by the extractive industries with 16%. There is a strong regional concentration of investment locations with North Africa and South Africa accounting for nearly half of all projects. Looking at the *number* of FDI projects, the main investors are the USA (18% of projects), the United Kingdom (10%), France (9%), followed by China (E&Y, 2018: 24). The main sources of FDI inflow by value are China and the Middle East accounting for more than 50% of investments (Analyze Africa 2017).

Turning to foreign trade, SSA is experiencing strong growth. Exports in goods and services grew at an average rate of 3.9% p.a. (2000–2019) while imports grew by 6.4% p.a. in the same period. The outlook from 2020 to 2024 is positive with exports and imports of goods and services both expected to grow at a rate of 5.3% and 4.5% p.a., respectively (IMF n.d.-b).[8] The centers of gravity of Africa's merchandise exports have shifted from Europe and the USA (−16% and −9.6 percentage points, respectively) to China and Asia (+9.3% and +14.2 percentage points, respectively). In general, Africa has diversified its regional export markets with China having caught up with the European Union and the USA to become the major trading region of Africa.[9] In 2017 African exports to China consisted of 79% fuels and mining products, which is a fairly stable share. These two facts—China becoming a major export destination and three quarters of exports to China being commodities—raises the challenge for SSA countries to move away from commodity-based exports in order to reduce their vulnerability to exogenous world market price shocks. Nonetheless, the overall trend of African exports to the world showed a distinct drop in the share of fuels and mining products from 59% in 2000 to 49.5% in 2017. The export shares of manufacturing and agriculture both rose, indicating ongoing diversification. Despite improvements, export diversification is still very limited as the diversification index shows.[10] On average, for all of Africa 11 product lines account for 75% of exports, with crude oil at 44% of the export value on average. Especially Central Africa and Western Africa show high concentration indices indicating a lasting export dependency on just a few products (mainly raw materials) (WTO n.d.). Southern Africa and Eastern Africa have fairly diversified export structures, which is an indication of a diversified economy (UNCTAD n.d.-c). This export development can be summarized as follows:

> Despite the substantial trade expansion, export diversification remains a challenge for Africa. The concentration of exports in a few commodities and sectors limits trade potential, undermines the capacity to create jobs and increases exposure to global economic shocks. (AfDB et al. 2017)

In the past years, imports have outgrown exports. The import structure of SSA was dominated by machinery (30%), fuels (16%), chemicals (12.4%), and food (12.1%) in 2018. Pharmaceuticals account for 2.9% of total imported merchandise goods. Imports into Sub-Saharan Africa as a region in 2018 stood at USD 340 billion with a long-term annual growth rate of 8.9% (CAGR 2000–2018) and a much lower medium-term growth of 2.1% per annum. This slowdown of growth rates is the

---

[8]Again, it has to be noted that the short-term forecast is overshadowed by the Covid-19 pandemic.

[9]The share of intra-African trade hovers at well below 20% of total exports. Despite various regional integration agreements across the continent there was little trade creation. There are two main causes for this: (1) the manufacturing base in Africa is very limited reducing the scope of products that can be traded; (2) many of the regional integration agreements do not work as well as planned (AfDB et al. 2017).

[10]The diversification index shows the number of export product lines accounting for more than 75% of total exports.

result of increasing domestic production in some industries and slowing economic activities in other regions since 2014. However, what is worrying is the under-proportionate import growth of productive goods. Especially machinery only grew at 0.9% per annum between 2010 and 2018 whereas, between 2000 and 2018, 17 of 47 SSA countries had double-digit annual import growth rates in machinery. The slowdown in machinery imports reduces future production capacity and keeps productivity low. This results in a lack of global competitiveness of SSA countries and obstructs deeper integration into Global Value Chains (GVC) (AfDB et al. 2014).

The chapter now turns to investigate the conditions for doing business in SSA as they directly influence the development of a business model that addresses the Bottom of the Pyramid market for pharmaceutical products.

4.3 Business Environment Conditions in Sub-Saharan Africa

Economic and political conditions are, on a macro-level, indirectly relevant for companies' interest in a country. More directly relevant is the actual market potential and the conditions for doing business which determine the operational ease (or difficulty) of seizing opportunities and turning them into sales and profit. Hence, a brief section on the operationally relevant market conditions in SSA is presented. In Chap. 5 the healthcare system and the pharmaceutical market in SSA are discussed in order to assess market attractiveness.

One high-level evaluation of the doing business conditions is provided in the rankings of the *Global Competitiveness Report* 2019 published by the World Economic Forum. Sub-Saharan Africa as a region shows a poor performance: No country is ranked in the top 50 countries (out of 141) and 17 countries are in the bottom 20. Of the large countries in SSA, South Africa is ranked 60, Kenya 97, and Nigeria 116. On the positive side, SSA is the second-fastest improving region after the Middle East and North Africa. The main fields of fast improvement are Information and Communication Technologies (ICT) adoption followed by healthcare provision and market size (WEF 2019b). A second high-level indication of the business environment is the more operational business-focused *Doing Business Report* 2020 (World Bank 2020). Overall, it finds similar results: 11 Sub-Saharan African countries are amongst the worst performing 20 countries worldwide (out of 190 countries). Despite various reforms that the SSA countries have introduced in the past, efforts have not been sufficient to lift them out of the lower rankings, since other world regions were either already far ahead or conducted more far-reaching reforms. This is why SSA as a region merely improved its Doing Business score compared to previous years but not its global position.

Obviously, the doing business conditions are very heterogeneous across countries. The best ranked SSA country is Mauritius (Rank 13, well ahead of Germany ranked 22 and China in 31st place), followed by Rwanda (38), Morocco (53), Kenya

(56), and South Africa (84). Looking at the top 10 reformer countries, Nigeria and Togo are among them. However, in the case of Nigeria, it is starting from the low rank of 131 and Togo from 97th place in the Ease of Doing Business rankings (World Bank 2020). An overview of the doing business conditions, grouped according to operational business activity, for selected countries is provided in Table 4.2. The most striking point is that only in relatively few criteria and countries did the doing business indicators worsen in the last 3 years (colored in the table). Only the indicators dealing with corruption and logistics/logistical infrastructure seem to have deteriorated between 2016 and 2019.

The following sections will discuss the doing business conditions clustered according to operational activities.

4.3.1 *Distribution and Logistics*

The most common market-entry strategy in the Sub-Saharan African markets is still via export to local distributors. These exporting companies are affected by the weak import-related conditions: Eight of the 48 Sub-Saharan African countries were in the top 100 of all ranked countries when it came to the cost and speed of importing and exporting (trading across borders) in 2019. Of these eight countries, none is a major SSA country. Countries like Kenya (117), South Africa (145), Ethiopia (156), Ghana (158), and Nigeria (179) rank toward the bottom of the ranking (out of 190 countries). SSA as a region ranks last in all cost and speed criteria when it comes to imports in global comparison (World Bank 2020).

Looking at more details and referring to Table 4.2, the logistical conditions in most SSA countries are inferior to those in China and Germany. "Trading across borders" performance in terms of import time and cost has remained stable but on a low level. Positive exceptions are Botswana (USD 98, 4 h), to some extent Ethiopia (USD 120, 72 h) and Namibia (USD 145, 6 h). All other countries are at least twice as expensive (going up to a factor of five in South Africa and Namibia) for border compliance costs and up to ten times slower than China (World Bank 2020). A big cost (and time) driver in international transportation is the low integration of all SSA countries into global shipping routes (Liner Shipping Connectivity Index). South Africa with the highest Connectivity Index of 34.6 stands at only 22% of China (152) and 40% of Germany (83) (UNCTAD n.d.-a). The overall quality of ports in SSA is amongst the lowest in the world, with few countries being rated comparable to China (4.6 out of 7): Namibia (5.2), South Africa (4.8), Kenya (4.5), and Senegal (4.4) (World Bank n.d.-c). However, when looking at the broad Logistical Performance Index (LPI), only South Africa (LPI of 3.4) is competitive with China (LPI of 3.6). Reasons for the average low rating of port efficiency (with the named exceptions) are low docking capacity, insufficient port storage capacity and quality, and outdated (often still mechanical) movement gear (Carlowitz and Röndigs 2016).

Table 4.2 Operational doing business indicators in selected SSA countries

		Value Generation - Distribution and Logistics KPIs							Value Capture: Selling and Finance KPIs					
	Year	Logistic Performance Index (LPI) (1=low, 5=high, 2016-2018)	Quality of Port Infrastructure Index (1=low, 7=high, 2016-2017)	Liner Ship. Connectivity Index (max. value in 2004 = 100)	Cost to export: Border compliance (USD)	Cost to import: Border compliance (USD)	Time to export: Border compliance (hours)	Time to import: Border compliance (hours)	Getting Credit total score (DB15-19 methodology)	Corruption Perception Index (2016/2018)	Paying Taxes - Time (hours p.a.)	Paying Taxes - Total tax rate (% of profit)	Enforcing Contracts - Time (days)	Enforcing Contracts - Cost (% of claim)
Angola	2019	2.0	n/a	25.9	825	1030	164	72	1	19	287	49.1	1296	44.4
	2016	2.2	n/a	23.4	825	1030	312	276	1	18	287	48	1296	44.4
Benin	2019	2.7	3.9	17.5	354	599	78	82	6	40	270	48.9	595	64.7
	2016	2.4	3.4	17.0	354	599	78	82	6	36	270	48.9	750	64.7
Botswana	2019	n/a	3.1	n/a	317	98	5	4	12	61	120	25.1	660	39.8
	2016	3.0	2.7	n/a	317	98	8	4	12	60	152	25.1	660	39.8
Burkina Faso	2019	2.6	n/a	n/a	261	265	75	102	6	41	270	41.3	446	81.7
	2016	2.7	n/a	n/a	261	265	75	102	6	42	270	41.3	446	81.7
Cameroon	2019	2.6	3.1	16.3	983	1407	202	271	12	25	624	57.7	800	46.6
	2016	2.2	3.3	17.1	983	1407	202	271	7	26	648	57.7	800	46.6
Côte d'Ivoire	2019	3.1	n/a	18.8	423	456	239	125	14	35	187	50.1	525	41.7
	2016	2.6	5.2	18.8	423	456	239	125	6	34	270	51.3	525	41.7
Ethiopia	2019	n/a	2.7	n/a	172	120	51	72	3	34	300	37.7	530	15.2
	2016	2.4	3.2	n/a	172	120	57	109	3	34	306	37.7	530	15.2
Ghana	2019	2.6	3.6	19.8	490	553	108	80	12	41	226	55.4	710	23
	2016	2.7	3.5	20.5	490	553	108	89	12	43	224	32.7	710	23
Kenya	2019	2.8	4.5	17.0	143	833	16	194	19	27	180	37.2	465	41.8
	2016	3.3	4.2	16.0	143	833	21	180	14	26	196	37.4	465	41.8
Mozambique	2019	n/a	3.6	12.1	602	399	66	9	5	23	200	36.1	950	53.3
	2016	2.7	3.6	11.1	602	399	78	14	5	27	200	36.1	950	53.3
Namibia	2019	n/a	5.2	15.4	745	145	120	6	12	53	302	20.7	460	35.8
	2016	2.7	5.2	16.0	745	145	120	6	12	52	302	20.7	460	35.8
Nigeria	2019	2.5	2.8	21.4	786	1077	128	242	17	27	343	34.8	399	38.9
	2016	2.6	3.0	22.6	786	1077	135	284	12	28	429	34.9	454	38.9
Rwanda	2019	3.0	2.9	n/a	183	282	83	74	19	56	91	33.2	230	64.6
	2016	3.0	3.3	n/a	183	282	97	86	18	54	124	33	230	65.3
Senegal	2019	2.3	4.4	16.6	547	702	62	53	13	45	416	44.8	650	36.4
	2016	2.3	4.1	17.2	547	702	62	53	6	45	441	45.1	925	36.4
South Africa	2019	3.4	4.8	34.6	1257	676	92	87	12	43	210	29.2	600	33.2
	2016	3.8	4.9	37.8	1257	668	92	87	12	45	203	28.8	600	33.2
Tanzania	2019	n/a	3.4	15.9	1175	1350	96	402	13	36	207	43.8	515	14.3
	2016	3.0	3.4	13.8	1175	1350	96	402	13	32	195	43.9	515	14.3
Uganda	2019	2.6	2.6	n/a	209	447	59	145	12	26	195	33.7	490	31.3
	2016	3.0	2.5	n/a	209	447	71	154	12	25	195	33.7	490	31.3
Zambia	2019	2.5	2.3	n/a	370	380	120	120	19	35	158	15.6	611	38.7
	2016	2.4	2.2	n/a	370	380	148	163	15	38	186	18.6	611	38.7
Zimbabwe	2019	2.1	3.1	n/a	285	562	88	228	13	22	242	31.6	410	83.1
	2016	2.1	3.2	n/a	285	562	88	228	10	22	242	31.6	410	83.1
Reference Countries														
China	2019	3.6	4.6	151.9	256	241	21	36	60	39	138	59.2	496	16.2
	2016	3.7	4.5	140.1	484	745	26	92	60	40	259	68.2	496	16.2
Germany	2019	4.2	5.5	82.8	345	0	36	0	70	80	218	48.8	499	14.4
	2016	4.2	5.6	83.5	345	0	36	0	70	81	218	48.9	499	14.4

negative clnage

Source: Own Illustration, based on World Bank (2020)

Turning to land-based logistics, road and rail densities in SSA remain to be the lowest of all world regions, making national logistics expensive and unreliable. Road density stands at 0.09 km of road per square kilometer of land area in 2011, down from 0.11 in 1990. Rail density is 0.002 km per square kilometers, half of what it was in 1990. As a proxy for the quality of roads, a look at the share of surfaced roads reveals only 17% of all roads showed an improvement between 2006 and 2015. According to perception, the rail quality in Sub-Saharan Africa also showed improvements between 2006 and 2015, yet it remains at the bottom of all world regions (World Bank 2017). In the shorter term, according to the World Economic Forum's Global Competitiveness Report 2017, the quality of roads has not improved in the past 4 years. It rather stagnated at a fairly low level: "The development of transport and energy infrastructure has stagnated, widening the gap with advanced economies and developing Asia" (WEF 2017). Similar developments are observed for air and rail transportation infrastructure. Thus, weak logistical conditions in essentially all SSA countries is caused by insufficient transport infrastructure in terms of quality and capacity (Arvis et al. 2018). The more current assessment is that the infrastructure situation in SSA is not only by far the worst worldwide but actually deteriorated from 2018 to 2019 (WEF 2019a, b). Looking at the finance gap for the infrastructure of over USD 100 bn per year (of a predicted need of USD 130–167 bn p.a.) as estimated by the African Development Bank this stagnation is likely to continue (AfDB 2018; WEF 2019a).

All of this means that, logistically, Sub-Saharan African markets are not easily, let alone cheaply, reached and served for trade purposes. Domestic logistics are no better. This substantially raises the logistics side of distribution costs and, equally important, reduces logistical reliability. This makes it more difficult and more expensive to ensure product availability for customers and to create an efficient value delivery system in the business model:

> Reliable transport infrastructure, in all of its four subsectors—roads, railways, air transport, and ports—is an essential component of all countries' competitiveness. [...] Reliable transport must be in place for companies to import and export goods, to fill orders, and to obtain supplies (WEF 2013).

4.3.2 Access to Finance

On the sales side, companies are facing challenges especially in the field of financing deals. The availability of funds, especially in foreign currency, is one of the many cited challenges of business (compare the studies by Carlowitz 2018, 2019). According to the World Bank's Doing Business Report 2020, Sub-Saharan Africa has the lowest score with regard to the criterion "getting credit" (see Table 4.2): Access to credit is 3–20 times easier in China than in the SSA countries. As a result, less than 10% of the population and businesses have taken out a loan in 80% of these countries in the past 5 years. This has consequences for investment and business (import) funding: 75% of investments in SSA are funded using own financial resources. The share of domestic credit (of all forms) extended to the private sector in GDP is limited. Only South Africa and Mauritius reach similar levels to China (157%).[11] All other countries range from 40% domestic credit as a share of GDP down to single-digit shares (for instance the Democratic Republic of Congo) or low double-digit values (for instance Tanzania) indicating weak domestic credit markets (World Bank n.d.-b). These values can mean several things in terms of financing business transactions: Much of the business is financed from customers' cash flow or income, some are received through informal credit channels, and some credit volumes might be external.

Additional insights can be gained when looking at the source of the loans people took out in 2017: Of the over-15-year-olds, 2% (Côte d'Ivoire) to 16% (Kenya) took out a loan from a financial institution in the past 12 months, which is roughly in line with China and Germany. However, the main source for loans in SSA is family and friends, which ranges between 20% and 45% of respondents (in China the corresponding figure is only 8.6%). Another fairly high share of respondents (between 2% and 9%) said they had taken out a loan from private lenders. In countries with a weak banking system (on average well below China's 8 bank branches per 100,000 inhabitants), the share of private and family lending is higher than that from financial institutions (World Bank n.d.-b). For nearly all countries in SSA, the lending interest rate is double digit (up to 60% in Madagascar and 38% in Malawi; for comparison: China 4.4% in 2017). One exception is the CFA-currency union countries in West Africa plus four additional countries that had single-digit lending rates (World Bank n.d.-d). The lending-deposit rate spread is, for the vast majority of countries, 2–3 times the level of China (World Bank n.d.-b). These numbers show that it is difficult and expensive for customers and companies to get credit. This limits the consumption capacity of potential customers and the ability of local distributors to finance their trading business, which impacts on the availability of products. However, for the population and local business access has improved via mobile money solutions and the cooperation of commercial banks with mobile money providers (Gosavi 2018). New financial sources are being created with an increasing number of "FinTechs" on the continent (compare Carlowitz 2020).

Linked to the issue of access to finance is the availability of foreign currency to pay for imported products. This is a problem in various SSA countries and can limit, on a country level, the growth potential by hindering the import of machinery or other productive goods. A survey conducted by The Economist amongst managers in Africa shows that hard currency availability and exchange rate fluctuation are the biggest operational business challenges (The Economist 2017). This is supported by a PWC (2017) survey amongst 80 CEOs running a business in Africa.

[11] A figure greater than 100% indicates relending of credit funds.

Table 4.3 Doing business indicators for localization in selected SSA countries

	Year	Days to Start a Business - Men	Cost to Start a Business - Men (% of income p. c.)	Min. capital to Start a Business (% of income p. c.)	Dealing with Construction Permits - Time (days)	Dealing w/ Construct. Permits - Cost (% of ware-house value)	Getting Electricity - Time (days)	Registering Property - Time (days)	Registering Property - Cost (% of property value)
Angola	2019	36	11.1	0	184	1	97	190	2.7
	2016	36	20.7	0	214	2	145	190	3.1
Benin	2019	8	3.4	5	88	4.8	90	120	3.4
	2016	8	3.7	5.4	88	5.2	90	120	11.5
Botswana	2019	48	0.6	0	102	0.4	77	27	5.1
	2016	48	0.8	0	106	0.5	77	12	5.1
Burkina Faso	2019	13	42.8	6.3	121	7.6	169	67	11.9
	2016	13	43.4	7	121	8.4	169	67	12.1
Cameroon	2019	13	24.6	12	126	17.6	64	81	13.7
	2016	16	32	137.6	135	18.9	64	86	18.8
Côte d'Ivoire	2019	6	2.7	2.7	163	5.9	53	39	7.1
	2016	7	18.9	3.3	373	6.6	55	30	7.6
Ethiopia	2019	32	45.4	0	136	12.6	95	52	6
	2016	35	69.3	121.5	149	19.7	95	52	6.1
Ghana	2019	13	12.3	1	170	3.5	55	33	6.1
	2016	14	19.7	2	170	6.2	79	33	6.1
Kenya	2019	23	22.4	0	159	2.8	97	43.5	5.9
	2016	22	28.2	0	160	6.1	97	61	6.1
Mozambique	2019	17	106.9	0	118	6	40	43	5
	2016	21	64.6	0	118	6.2	77	43	5.8
Namibia	2019	54	8.9	0	160	2	37	44	13.8
	2016	66	11.5	0	160	2.5	37	52	13.8
Nigeria	2019	7	26.1	0	105	4	110	92	11.3
	2016	25	31.3	0	105	24.8	149	92	11.3
Rwanda	2019	4	0	0	97	11.4	30	7	0.1
	2016	4	48.5	0	113	14.1	34	12	0.1
Senegal	2019	6	22.6	3	177	7.8	68	41	7.1
	2016	6	62.7	4.7	177	10.4	75	71	10.2
South Africa	2019	40	0.2	0	155	1.9	109	23	8
	2016	45	0.2	0	155	1.9	109	23	7.3
Tanzania	2019	29.5	40.6	0	184	5.4	105	67	5.2
	2016	29	54	0	236	7.4	109	67	4.4
Uganda	2019	24	40.5	0	113	7.4	66	42	3.9
	2016	26	46.1	0	122	9	66	42	2.6
Zambia	2019	8.5	34	0	188	2.3	117	45	9.5
	2016	8.5	34.7	0	188	3.3	117	45	9.9
Zimbabwe	2019	27	76.6	0	178	12.6	106	29	7.3
	2016	91	121.5	0	238	25.4	106	36	7.6
Reference Countries									
China	2019	9	1.1	0	111	2.8	32	9	4.6
	2016	27	1.6	0	266	8.2	143	23	4.9
Germany	2019	8	6.5	29.8	126	1.1	28	52	6.6
	2016	8	6.7	32.9	126	1.2	28	52	6.7

negative change   p.c. = per capita

Source: Own Illustration, based on World Bank (2020)

4.3.3 *Conditions Relevant When Localizing Business*

When the mode of market entry is to establish a subsidiary (or sales representation), additional location-related factors become relevant, of which most have improved between 2016 and 2019 (compare Table 4.3). In 2019, starting a business in SSA took on average more working days than in Germany (8 days) or China (9 days). However, there are some countries that are equally fast or faster (e.g., 4 days in Rwanda, 6 days in Senegal and Côte d'Ivoire). The cost of starting a business as a percentage of per capita income is significantly higher on average. However, some exceptions exist, for instance, countries such as Rwanda, South Africa, and Botswana that charge less than 1% of GDP per capita (China 1.1%). In addition, there are country-specific regulations, for instance, in Ghana, a minimum of USD 1 million equity and the employment of at least 20 local employees is a prerequisite for establishing a legal entity (AHK Ghana 2018). This creates obstacles to building a local presence, especially given the small market sizes. In general, for most countries in SSA, bureaucratic challenges exist in the field of taxes, license obtainment (operation, work permits, etc.), and inefficiencies in the application process, e.g., construction permits, getting electricity, etc. (World Bank n.d.-a).

When localizing a business, the need for qualified employees becomes directly relevant. In 2018, people in SSA spend on average only 6 years in school, (in all other regions in the world the figure is at least 9 years) and annual spending per pupil in primary school is USD 533 (25% of Latin America's and 20% of Asia's spending) and in secondary school, it is USD 925 per pupil and year (50% of Latin America spending and 20% of Asia's level) (AfDB 2020). Looking at the quality of education, one important driver is the pupil-teacher ratio: In SSA, for secondary schools, it averaged 21.6 in 2018 and ranged from 8.3 (Comoros) to 72.3 (Malawi) students per teacher (in Germany in 2018 it was 12). In primary education, the SSA average stood at 37.4 students-per-teacher with a range of 14.5 (Seychelles) to 59.5 (Rwanda) (World Bank n.d.-d). Another education quality indicator is the number of pupils per book: In 2015 the average number for SSA was 3 students per mathematics book (ranging from 13 in Cameroon to less than 1 in various other countries) and 2 students per reading textbook (ranging from 12 in Cameroon to less than 1 for many other countries) (UNESCO 2016). These unfavorable conditions resulted in low test scores in 2016 ranging from 300 to 625 points with an SSA average of 374 as opposed to a world average of upper middle-income countries of 431. This low performance of the education system makes it necessary for companies to train their new hires and employees. However, only in two countries (Botswana and Rwanda) are more than 40% of all companies involved in training employees. In all other countries companies are well below that level. For comparison, in China, the figure is around 80% of companies. The reason for this low level of training is the issue of retention and the problem of competitors "poaching" skilled labor (AfDB 2020). Translating all of these facts into a business logic shows that it is difficult to get qualified managers and technically well-trained staff for after-sales services. This shortage is one of the reasons for the low and stagnant productivity in Sub-Saharan African economies (WEF 2017) which makes them—combined with small market sizes—fairly unattractive for production.

4.3.4 Conclusion on Doing Business Conditions

Companies face challenges on all levels of business activities when doing business in SSA. Especially since the localization of some business activities is fairly important, the—in places—harsh business environment throws up a wide range of obstacles to companies. Dealing with these conditions is often costly and leads to rising prices for consumers (e.g., high logistics costs). Having said that, there is also a notable improvement in doing business conditions across SSA countries and across operational activity fields despite the vast majority of the countries remaining at the bottom of the rankings. The business environment remains significantly different from the one that multinational companies are used to from developed markets. This needs to be considered in business model innovation (see Sect. 3.1). When looking at the doing business conditions specifically in BoP markets the situation can be expected to be even worse than described in this chapter.

4.4 Bottom of the Pyramid in Sub-Saharan Africa

Detailed information on the specifics of BoP markets in Sub-Saharan Africa are hard to find despite a large number of hits in Google Scholar for the search string *Africa "Bottom of the Pyramid"* (15,400 hits in total and 5490 hits as of 2015). The papers found focused on specific business topics in the BoP segment neither providing information on the size and structure of the market nor offering specific consumer behavior analysis.

Following the income definition of the BoP from Sect. 2.1, the following sizes for the BoP segment and its sub-segments can be calculated as shown in Fig. 4.5.

The non-BoP population with more than USD 2000 (2011 PPP) annual income exhibited a disproportionate increase with a CAGR of 6.0% between 2002 and 2015, which corresponds to the idea of a growing middle class. The size of the BoP market in SSA was 856 million people in 2015 which is an annual growth of 2.3%. This relatively low growth rate is driven by the efforts to eradicate extreme poverty (<USD 1.90, 2011 PPP) which grew at a mere 0.6% p.a. This positive growth in absolute numbers might be confusing as the share of people in extreme poverty to the

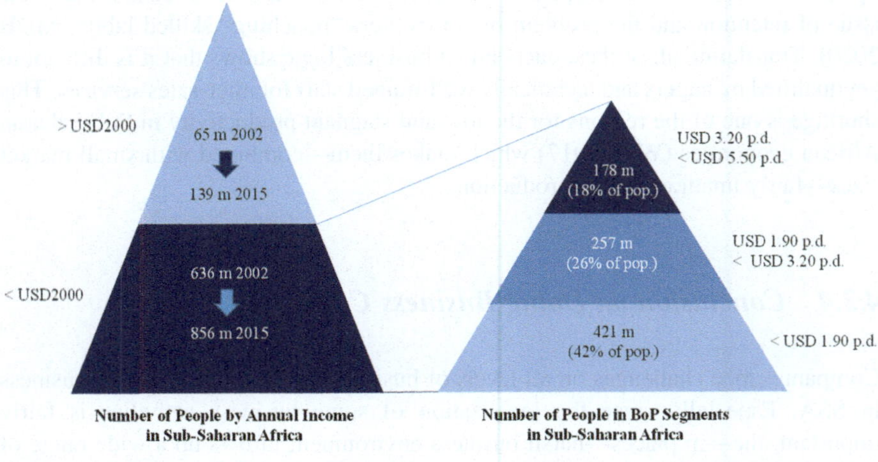

Fig. 4.5 BoP segments by population and income in SSA 2015 (USD, 2011 PPP). Source: Own Illustration, based on World Bank (n.d.-d)

total population has declined from 55.4% to 42.3%. However, due to population growth of 2.7% p.a., the *absolute* poverty figures, which here correspond to the definition of BoP, have increased. As discussed above, from a multinational pharmaceutical company's point of view, the relevant and addressable BoP segment lies between USD 1.90 (2011, PPP) and USD 5.50 per day. This addressable BoP segment in SSA has an estimated market size of 430 million people. It has been growing much faster than that of extreme poverty with an annual growth rate for the segment USD 1.90–3.20 per day (2011, PPP) of 4% and for the market segment of USD 3.20–5.50 per day (2011, PPP) of 5.2%. Estimates of the BoP market size in USD including the entire BoP segment vary depending on the definition but all show significant numbers. A study by Hammond and Kramer (2007) saw the BoP market in all of Africa as standing at approximately USD 430 bn in 2007, which is based on a definition of annual income below USD 3000. The author's own calculations based on the World Bank's poverty level data only for the addressable BoP segment of USD 1.90–5.50 per day (2011, PPP) show a market size between USD 386 bn and USD 658 bn (own calculations, based on World Bank n.d.-d).[12] Therefore, the relevant BoP market has an attractive size and growth rates, despite each individual customer's limited purchasing power, and it is in this way that it needs to be considered in the business model (Pitta et al. 2008).

There is limited structural information on the BoP market in Africa, especially when it comes to customer profiles. Most of the aspects discussed in Sect. 2.2 also describe the BoP market and customer characteristics in SSA. They are: low income, insufficient physical infrastructure to reach the BoP, low level of education, and thus limited market transparency (despite increasing ICT penetration). BoP customers are difficult to access whether they are in rural areas (see the low urbanization rate in Sub-Saharan Africa) or in slums. In addition, institutional, governance, and doing business topics that were presented throughout this chapter provide additional insights at a country level.

4.5 Conclusion

The political situation in SSA as a region is improving but the situation remains volatile in most countries especially since the population is dissatisfied with political performance, and trust in political stakeholders is limited. Especially problematic is the rule of law, specifically on the execution side, as the population has little trust in the police. The population has significant policy-related concerns including on health and poverty. The economic development outlook of SSA still depends on external factors. Most notably, the high dependency of major economies on

[12]The range was calculated by multiplying the number of people in each income segment with (a) the lower value of the respective range (USD 1.90–3.20 and USD 3.20–5.50) and (b) with the higher value of each range. Then the two segment USD-values were added to give the shown range.

commodity exports impacts the continent's development directly in terms of vulnerability to world market price fluctuations. This has a direct impact on the economies' development via their trade balance but also via indirect effects such as low foreign exchange earnings and generation of tax revenue. Also, FDI significantly impacts economic growth and needs to be considered. Especially countries' investments—of which, for some countries, FDI is a large proportion—were found to be important for diversification efforts as they increase a country's competitiveness through rising productivity as much as through knowledge and technology transfer. In general, it is important to note that the dependence on external factors is still high but has been declining in recent years. Regarding doing business conditions, SSA is improving but remains at the bottom of all rankings with some exceptions. Regardless of market entry mode, the business environment is challenging and will remain so in the forseeable future.

The socioeconomic aspects in SSA related to the BoP read as follows: a high rate of poverty, high Gini coefficient, significant slum building, and a large proportion of rural population indicate two issues relevant for business: (1) The BoP market in SSA is attractive by size in customer numbers and in aggregated USD terms. However, individual purchasing power is low. (2) Access to many of these low-income consumers is difficult as they are dispersed. These two factors make distribution a major challenge. Challenges addressing the BoP in SSA are further aggravated by doing business conditions that are among the worst in the world as well as being heterogeneous across the different countries. Despite the challenging conditions, profits *are* made by international companies. Therefore, Sub-Saharan Africa is obviously an excellent use case to analyze how to successfully address the BoP, as the region fits the circumstances and conditions that the BoP literature describes. The following chapter will describe the healthcare system and situation as well as the pharmaceutical industry in SSA.

References

AfDB (2018) African Economic Outlook 2018. Abidjan

AfDB (2019) African Economic Outlook 2019. Abidjan

AfDB (2020) African economic African economic outlook 2020 - developing Africa's developing Africa's workforce for the future. African Development Bank, Abidjan

AfDB (n.d.) AFDB Socio Economic Database, 1960-2020. http://dataportal.opendataforafrica.org/nbyenxf/afdb-socio-economic-database-1960-2020. Accessed 5 Apr 2020

AfDB, OECD, UNDP (2014) African Economic Outlook 2014. OECD, Paris

AfDB, OECD, UNDP (2017) African Economic Outlook 2017. OECD, Paris

Afrika Verein der Deutschen Wirtschaft e.V. (2015) Jahr der Entscheidung. Berlin. https://www.afrikaverein.de/. Accessed 15 Aug 2018

Afrobarometer (n.d.) The online data analysis tool (R7 2016/2018). http://afrobarometer.org/online-data-analysis/analyse-online. Accessed 24 Jan 2018

AHK Ghana (2018) Interview about relevant conditions when localizing business in Ghana on 28 Apr 2018

Analyze Africa (2017) The Africa Investment Report 2017. http://africabusiness2020.com/2017/10/15/free-download-africa-investment-report-2017/. Accessed 27 Apr 2018
Arvis J-F, Ojala L, Wiederer C, Shepherd B, Raj A, Dairabayeva K, Kiiski T (2018) Connecting to compete 2018. Trade logistics in the global economy. The Logistics Performance Index and its indicators. World Bank, Washington, DC. https://openknowledge.worldbank.org/handle/10986/29971. Accessed 12 Aug 2019
Bello-Schünemann J, D Moyer J (2018) Structural pressures and political instability: trajectories for sub-Saharan Africa. Africa Report 9, Institute for Security Studies. https://journals.co.za/content/journal/10520/ejc-1486c2afe3?crawler=true&mimetype=application/pdf. Accessed 26 Mar 2019
Carlowitz Pv (2020) Digitalisierung in den Zukunftsmärkten Subsahara Afrikas-Chancen und Geschäftsmodelle für österreichische Unternehmen Bundesministerium Digitalisierung und Wirtschaftsstandort Österreich, Wien
Coface (2020) Country & Sector Risks Handbook 2020. Paris. http://downloads.coface.com/CofaceHandbook2020. Accessed 5 Apr 2020
Credendo (2020) Country risk and insights. https://www.credendo.com/country-risk. Accessed 23 Feb 2020
Economist Intelligence Unit (2019) Country profiles, London
EY (2018) Global analysis of health insurance in Sub-Saharan Africa. https://www.ey.com/Publication/vwLUAssets/EY-global-analysis-of-health-insurance-in-sub-saharan-africa/%24File/ey-global-analysis-of-health-insurance-in-sub-saharan-africa.pdf. Accessed 12 Feb 2020
Globalintegrity (2018) Africa integrity indicators 2018. https://www.globalintegrity.org/resource/aii6-xls/. Accessed 8 Mar 2020
Gosavi A (2018) Can mobile money help firms mitigate the problem of access to finance in Eastern sub-Saharan Africa? J Afr Bus 19:343–360
Hammond AL, Kramer W (2007) The next 4 Billion: market size and business strategy at the base of the pyramid. World Resources Institute, Washington, DC
IMF (n.d.-a) World Economic Outlook Database. April 2020 edition. https://www.imf.org/external/pubs/ft/weo/2020/01/weodata/index.aspx. Accessed 15 Apr 2020
IMF (n.d.-b) World Economic Outlook Database. October 2019 edition. https://www.imf.org/external/pubs/ft/weo/2020/01/weodata/index.aspx. Accessed 15 Apr 2020
IMF (2020) Regional economic outlook: Subsahara Africa. COVID-19- an unprecedented threat to development. International Monetary Fund, Washington, DC
Pitta DA, Guesalaga R, Marshall P (2008) The quest for the fortune at the bottom of the pyramid: potential and challenges. J Consum Mark 25:393–401
PWC (2017) The Africa business agenda. Changing gear, Price Waterhouse Cooper
The Economist (2017) 2017 African business outlook survey. The long view: reflections on commercial performance and prospects Johannesburg
UN (2019) World urbanization prospects: the 2018 revision. United Nations, New York
UNCTAD (2019) World investment report 2019. UNCTAD, New York
UNCTAD (n.d.-a) Liner Shipping Connectivity Index. http://unctadstat.unctad.org/wds/TableViewer/tableView.aspx?ReportId=92. Accessed 24 Mar 2018
UNCTAD (n.d.-b) National Account Statistics. UNCTAD STAT. http://unctadstat.unctad.org/wds/ReportFolders/reportFolders.aspx. Accessed 16 Aug 2018
UNCTAD (n.d.-c) Statistical Database. https://unctadstat.unctad.org/EN/. Accessed 23 Feb 2020
UNDP (2019) Human Development Report 2019: Beyond income, beyond averages, beyond today: inequalities in human development in the 21st century. New York
UNDP (n.d.) Human Development Index. http://hdr.undp.org/en/composite/HDI. Accessed 21 Oct 2018
UNECA (2019) Economic report on Africa 2019: Fiscal policy for financing sustainable development in Africa. Economic Commission for Africa. Addis Ababa
UNESCO (2016) School resources and learning environment in Africa - key results from a regional survey on factors affecting quality of education. http://uis.unesco.org/sites/default/files/school-

resources-and-learning-environment-in-africa-2016-en/school-resources-and-learning-environment-in-africa-2016-en.pdf. Accessed 5 Apr 2020

UN-HABITAT (2016) World Cities Report 2016. Urbanization and development: emerging futures. United Nations Human Settlements Programme. Nairobi

von Carlowitz P (2018) Chancen in Subsahara Afrika nutzen. Studie im Auftrag des Ministeriums für Wirtschaft, Arbeit und Wohnungsbau Baden-Württemberg

von Carlowitz P (2019) Geschäftsmodelle für Subsahara Afrika: Empirische Untersuchung der österreichischen Wirtschaft. WKO Fachreport – Wirtschaftskammer Österreich, Wien

von Carlowitz P, Röndigs A (2016) Distribution in Afrika. Distributionslogistik in Westafrika als Beispiel. Springer Gabler, Wiesbaden

WEF (2013) The Africa Competitiveness Report 2013. World Economic Forum, Geneva

WEF (2017) The Africa Competitiveness Report 2017. World Economic Forum, Geneva

WEF (2019a) Regional Risks for Doing Business 2019. World Economic Forum, Geneva

WEF (2019b) The Global Competitiveness Report 2019. World Economic Forum, Geneva

World Bank (2017) Africa's Pulse No. 15: An analysis of issues shaping Africa's economic future. World Bank, Washington, DC

World Bank (2020) Doing Business 2020: Comparing business regulation in 190 economies, 17th edn. The World Bank, Washington, DC

World Bank (n.d.-a) Enterprise Surveys Data. http://www.enterprisesurveys.org/data. Accessed 26 Mar 2018

World Bank (n.d.-b) Global Financial Indicators. http://databank.worldbank.org/data/reports.aspx?source=global-financial-development. Accessed 5 Apr 2020

World Bank (n.d.-c) Logistics Performance Index. https://lpi.worldbank.org/. Accessed 10 Aug 2018

World Bank (n.d.-d) World Development Indicator Database. https://data.worldbank.org/products/wdi. Accessed 4 Aug 2018

WTO (n.d.) Statistic database – Time series on international trade. https://timeseries.wto.org/. Accessed 17 Jan 2018

Chapter 5
Healthcare System and Pharmaceutical Market in Sub-Saharan Africa

Healthcare coverage is one of the 17 *Sustainable Development Goals (SDGs)* of the Agenda 2030 of the United Nations. Goal 3.8 SDG states:

> Achieve universal health coverage, including financial risk protection, access to quality essential health-care services, medicines and vaccines for all. (UN 2015)

The situation in SSA is bleak: There is a lack of coverage and quality of service and finance. Also, the high share of out-of-pocket spending contributes to poverty while poor health conditions are an important reason for low labor productivity and low competitiveness. Acknowledging all this, the African Union drew up the *African Health Strategy (AHS) 2016–2030*:

> [. . .] the goal of AHS 2016–2030 is to ensure healthy lives and promote the well-being for all in Africa in the context of "Agenda 2063: The Africa We Want" and the Sustainable Development Goals. The overall objective is to strengthen health systems performance, increase investments in health, improve equity and address social determinants of health to reduce priority diseases burden by 2030. (African Union 2016)

All efforts acknowledge that a functioning healthcare system consists of the service aspect and the physical aspect, of which one key element is pharmaceuticals. With an eye on the target of Universal Health Coverage, an increasing number of authors advocate embedding pharmaceutical production considerations into the healthcare system in lesser developed countries. The argument is straightforward: ensuring universal health coverage access to medicine is an integral part. Therefore, local pharmaceutical production is considered necessary to raise access to medicine, which improves the healthcare system and coverage (see Mackintosh et al. 2018; Gebre-Mariam et al. 2016; Russo and Banda 2015).

This interlinking of the healthcare system and policy on the one hand and pharmaceutical industry on the other makes it necessary to begin our analysis with a brief overview of the healthcare structures in SSA. Then the study will turn to the pharmaceutical market in order to understand the situation and challenges that exist and how these affect the aim of supplying the BoP market with medicines.

P. von Carlowitz, *Success in the Bottom of the Pyramid Market in Africa*,
SpringerBriefs in Business, https://doi.org/10.1007/978-3-030-59068-0_5

5.1 Healthcare System and Structure

In its report on global healthcare the Economist Intelligence Unit critically points out that "coverage" is not the same as "access" and that, especially with regard to access, it is the lower-income countries that struggle to guarantee it (The Economist 2017b). Access implies a good quality of healthcare, financial means, and physical access to healthcare facilities. Looking at the *Global Access to Healthcare Index* for the Sub-Saharan African countries, the top two ranked countries are South Africa ranking 43rd and Mozambique ranking 49th out of the 60 countries covered in the global index (The Economist 2017a). Another important index on the quality of the healthcare sector is the *Global Health Security Index* 2019, which looks at the health-related aspects of detection, prevention, response, sufficiency, commitment, and risk environment. In the index's ranking for 2019, only four SSA countries were above the average (South Africa, Kenya, Uganda, Ethiopia). Looking at the sub-index of "sufficient and robust health sector to treat the sick" only two SSA countries (South Africa and Ethiopia) ranked above the global average (Cameron et al. 2019). These ranks imply fundamental challenges in the healthcare system of nearly all SSA countries. This chapter will look at the healthcare system in Sub-Saharan Africa as this is a determinant of the BoP population's access to healthcare service and medicine. The architecture of the healthcare system determines the structure of expenditure on drugs, which is a key element of this book's analysis.

5.1.1 Healthcare Systems and Their Relevance

Access to good healthcare services is a key concern from an economic point of view. UNECA (2019) mentions various ways of how up to 25% of a country's economic growth can be attributed to a healthy population. Thus, the role of a strong healthcare system is economically important. Conversely, analyzing the economic cost of malnutrition and pandemic diseases, various studies show a significant negative impact. Despite the malnutrition level of SSA having declined over the past 20 years, it is still equivalent to the global level of 1995. Hence, the consequences of malnutrition via reduced productivity on GDP remain significant. Estimates of GDP reduction vary between 2 and 3% (World Bank), 11% (AfDB), and 16% (World Food Program) for the most affected countries. With regard to the GDP impact of pandemics illnesses such as tuberculosis, malaria, and HIV, various institutions have found equally significant effects. It is not just the direct effect on productivity that reduces GDP. There are additional negative indirect burdens on economic performance such as reduced tax revenues, a negative impact on tourism, and an increased strain on foreign exchange reserves through the extended need to import pharmaceuticals. Taking these aspects into account, the *African Economic Outlook* 2017 sees the cost of setting up a functioning health system as relatively small (AfDB et al. 2017). Going beyond the economic impact, there is a positive link between access to healthcare and human development: a positive correlation between the *Global Access to Healthcare Index* and the UNDP's *Human Development Index* has been discovered (The Economist 2017b). Thus, healthcare and living standards are positively linked.

Healthcare systems differ between countries: funds for the healthcare system are collected in many different ways (e.g., general tax revenues, earmarked taxes, mandatory or voluntary health insurance contributions), responsibilities of health funding management differs (e.g., Ministry of Health, local governments, a single public agency, or multiple health insurance funds), as well as consumer health services payment systems (e.g., budget allocations to government providers or payment to public and private providers for specific services) (World Bank 2016). Because of this variety, it is not feasible to detail each system in each country. Most challenges are related to quality (in most cases only basic health services are insured), quantity, and efficiency of the systems. If these issues are addressed by the government and it accepts the role of primary financier of universal health coverage in the country, a growing inflow of private investment into the healthcare system is expected (Mohandas 2019). Authors have also argued that universal healthcare coverage can only be achieved with strong government-sponsored insurance schemes. The *National Insurance Hospital Fund (NHIS)* in Kenya managed to cover approximately 50% of Kenyans in 2018. Apart from this example, few others exist.

It is not just the donor organizations and governments that focus on healthcare. A 2016 survey on coverage of, and access to, healthcare in 36 countries across Africa (Armah-Attoh et al. 2016) resulted in the following statements:

- Health clinics exist in about 75% of urban areas but only in 53% of rural areas.
- Nearly 50% of interviewees said they had gone without medical treatment at least once in the past year, which is a 10% drop from 10 years ago.
- Approximately half the population (46%) assess government efforts to provide access to basic healthcare to be insufficient: a worsening of 13 percentage points from 10 years ago.

The survey indicates some positive developments as a result of government efforts to improve the healthcare situation. At the same time, it shows there is still a long way to go to achieve the ultimate aim of Universal Healthcare Coverage.

5.1.2 Healthcare Service System Availability and Readiness

The World Health Organization (WHO) uses *Service Availability and Readiness Assessment* (SARA) in healthcare as a concept to assess the quality of a healthcare system. Service readiness refers to the quality and safety of healthcare, while service availability refers to access to healthcare and which health services are offered.

Table 5.1 General healthcare service readiness

Readiness domain	Basic amenities	Basic equipment	Standard precautions for infection, prevention and control	Diagnostics	Essential medicines	General service readiness index
Benin 2015	64	86	84	51	41	**65**
Burkina Faso 2014	72	89	88	61	38	**70**
Burundi 2017	71	79	73	52	29	**61**
Chad 2015	48	82	78	31	44	**57**
DRC 2014	n.d.	75	58	27	20	**45**
Ethiopia 2016	44	63	41	39	26	**43**
Kenya 2016	83	76	76	n.d.	73	**77**
Liberia 2016	77	57	73	42	44	**59**
Mauritania 2016	61	83	71	32	35	**56**
Niger 2015	64	82	75	36	41	**60**
Seychelles 2017	96	88	92	41	63	**76**
Sierra Leone 2017	57	77	83	33	31	**56**
Tanzania 2016	56	64	71	n.d.	n.d.	**64**
Togo 2013	49	87	85	40	39	**60**
Uganda 2013	62	79	83	47	35	**61**
Zambia 2015	71	87	89	66	43	**71**
Zimbabwe 2015	81	88	84	68	48	**74**
Regional Average	**66**	**78.9**	**76.7**	**44.4**	**40.6**	**62**

Percentage of items available that are considered essential by the WHO to provide the service (2013–2017)
Source: Based on WHO (2018)

Starting with general healthcare service readiness the WHO found large variations for the 17 African countries investigated. Kenya has the highest score of 77 (out of 100) while Ethiopia only scores 43 with regard to the essential items for general healthcare service readiness. The value for essential medicine and diagnostic equipment is even lower (Ethiopia scores 23 and Democratic Republic of Congo 27) while only the Seychelles (63) reached a level above 50 (WHO 2017a). Table 5.1

shows the readiness of the healthcare systems for general healthcare services by sub-group for the 17 SSA countries surveyed.

Overall, the general service readiness stood at 62 with regard to what the WHO deems necessary in terms of quality and safety standards. Higher scores were achieved in basic and standard services while the readiness level for diagnostic services (44.4) and essential medicines (40.6) was below average (WHO 2018). Thus, especially with respect to pharmaceutical products, there is a gap in readiness. The differences between healthcare systems across SSA becomes obvious when one looks at the range of values in Table 5.1.

The second aspect of a strong healthcare system is service availability, meaning easy access and variety of services offered. There are also significant differences between countries and healthcare services as Table 5.2 shows.

Access to services also depends on the type of services in question. The more basic health services are fairly well covered in the countries surveyed while more specialized services such as cancer screening and blood transfusion are less well covered. However, the survey found those services were provided in higher-end facilities which are usually not accessible to the poor.

Box 5.1. How do Citizens Assess the Healthcare System? (Afrobarometer n.d.)[1]

According to the surveys conducted by Afrobarometer over the past 10 years, the share of people with good access to medical care has increased in nearly all countries by double-digit percentages between the 2006/2007 and the 2014/2015 surveys. In Botswana, Ghana, Kenya, Mali, Namibia, Nigeria, and South Africa between 70% and 85% of surveyed people stating that obtaining access to medical care is easy. Some countries have also experienced strong improvements, with around half their population rating access as easy (for instance Senegal, Mozambique, Malawi, Côte d'Ivoire, and Benin). In terms of speed of access to medical care, most of the eight countries see their access as rather fast. Only in Malawi, Zimbabwe, and Uganda do a majority of the population rate access to medical aid as slow. In most countries, with the exception of Malawi and Zimbabwe, the majority of the population has seen an improvement in access to medical care in recent years. Naturally, survey results are not hard facts, but nonetheless, they provide a good overview of the prevailing sentiment. On average a positive development in the healthcare position is perceived, even if the level tends to be low.

The coverage of basic healthcare service (e.g., HIV, tuberculosis) still has gaps in the system in some countries. One main reason for the relatively low availability of

[1]The Afrobarometer surveys eight SSA countries on a regular basis. They are: Benin, Côte d'Ivoire, Kenya, Malawi, Mali, Uganda, Zambia, Zimbabwe. In each country more than 1000 citizens are interviewed.

Table 5.2 Healthcare services availability by type

	Benin 2015	Burkina Faso 2014	Burundi 2017	Chad 2015	DRC 2014	Ethiopia 2016	Kenya 2016	Liberia 2016	Mauritania 2016	Niger 2015	Seychelles 2017	Sierra Leone 2017	Tanzania 2016	Togo 2013	Uganda 2013	Zambia 2015	Zimbabwe 2015	Regional Average
Family planning	83	91	74	80	33	94	84	88	67	96	76	96	80	84	92	87	90	**82**
Antenatal care	91	90	71	96	78	80	89	90	72	93	48	97	85	93	70	90	91	**84**
Basic obstetric care	90	88	78	92	12	55	n.d.	89	69	89	16	96	76	91	53	69	89	**72**
Child immunization	78	86	64	91	75	80	85	82	65	92	68	95	81	89	77	89	93	**82**
Preventive and curative services	98	97	92	97	88	91	23	94	78	98	76	98	98	99	93	95	97	**89**
Adolescent health services	90	98	34	96	17	60	23	88	32	76	60	89	n.d.	90	59	62	89	**66**
Malaria	100	100	98	100	99	81	50	97	90	100	n.d.	100	99	100	100	100	96	**94**
TB	8	92	32	96	30	63	50	21	24	39	48	14	12	37	42	62	94	**45**
HIV counseling and testing	54	94	75	56	21	54	n.d.	52	12	63	n.d.	62	81	47	77	97	93	**63**
HIV care and support	26	88	38	35	9	29	n.d.	16	4	21	32	33	64	34	54	75	95	**41**
Diabetes	23	46	49	51	14	22	n.d.	22	27	29	n.d.	11	52	35	34	58	67	**36**
Cardiovascular diseases	25	86	45	28	16	41	n.d.	43	33	42	n.d.	20	65	45	44	72	73	**45**
Chronic obstructive respiratory disease	20	80	39	52	n.d.	45	n.d.	32	34	43	n.d.	15	61	36	48	73	73	**47**
Cervical cancer screening	9	21	3	n.d.	n.d.	2	n.d.	4	8	3	n.d.	3	n.d.	n.d.	n.d.	9	13	**8**
Basic surgery	65	98	75	100	71	52	n.d.	36	65	71	68	59	n.d.	31	54	73	55	**65**
Blood transfusion	7	5	6	7	15	4	44	n.d.	5	8	n.d.	4	n.d.	8	7	11	19	**11**
Comprehensive surgery	69	72	9	100	98	97	n.d.	81	100	90	50	87	n.d.	70	100	24	75	**75**
Service availability index	**59**	**80**	**53**	**68**	**46**	**52**	**59**	**58**	**46**	**61**	**52**	**59**	**69**	**61**	**62**	**71**	**76**	**59**

Percent of facilities that reported offering services, by service type(2013–2017)
Source: Based on WHO (2018)

services is a lack of medical workers. With only 14.1 skilled health professionals per 10,000 inhabitants, Africa has by far the lowest density of nurses and doctors in the world (South East Asia by comparison has 24.6, the world average stands at 52.8). In 13 of the 47 SSA countries, there are fewer than five skilled health professionals per 10,000 inhabitants (UNECA 2019). The situation is further exacerbated by a strong urban bias of healthcare professionals, leaving the rural poor exposed to health issues (Willcox et al. 2015). The cause of this limited coverage (and the low quality) in the healthcare system are the result of both a lack of funding and inefficiencies in the system (Musango and Ota 2015). Further, most countries' education systems have an "exceptionally low" graduation rate of medical workers with a bias toward higher-income countries on the African continent (Strasser et al. 2016). This also explains why the inequality in healthcare service coverage, even if declining slightly, remains high across African countries (World Bank 2016).

When looking at the regional averages of both tables, it becomes apparent that healthcare system service readiness and availability is (a) diverse across countries, and (b) acceptable in the more basic services (e.g., family planning) and weak in more advanced fields (e.g., diagnostics, cancer screening).

5.1.3 Healthcare System Funding

The key challenge regarding access to the healthcare system is financing the services in order to extend healthcare service coverage (The Economist 2017a). Whereas in Europe extensive (public) health insurance systems exist, the situation is fundamentally different in Africa. Public or private healthcare insurance covers less than 5% of total healthcare expenditure (WHO 2018). On average, in 2017 the countries in SSA spent 5.2% of their GDP on healthcare, a figure which has not changed since the year 2000. The level of spending on healthcare as a share of GDP varies significantly across the continent, with Gabon spending only 2.8%, while Sierra Leone spends 13.4% of GDP (World Bank n.d.-b). The rate of change has been diverse across countries with a decline of 4.9 percentage points in Comoros (still a fairly high level in 2017) to an increase of 6.3 percentage points in Malawi in 2017. The United Nations found a financing shortfall of USD66 bn per annum in the healthcare system in Sub-Saharan Africa if the target of basic healthcare coverage for 90% of the population is to be achieved (UNECA 2019). Out-of-pocket spending will remain a key feature of the healthcare funding until this shortfall is met by governments. The contribution of the four main sources of funding of the healthcare system in Sub-Saharan Africa is shown in Fig. 5.1.

Most African governments see healthcare and health insurance as a key policy topic. Usually these two areas have above-average spending shares of total government expenditure. Most countries have some sort of "National Health Plan or Scheme" in place (see for instance EY 2018; The Economist 2017a). For Sub-Saharan Africa in general and for the majority of countries, the main source of funding for healthcare provision remains public funding. Many countries

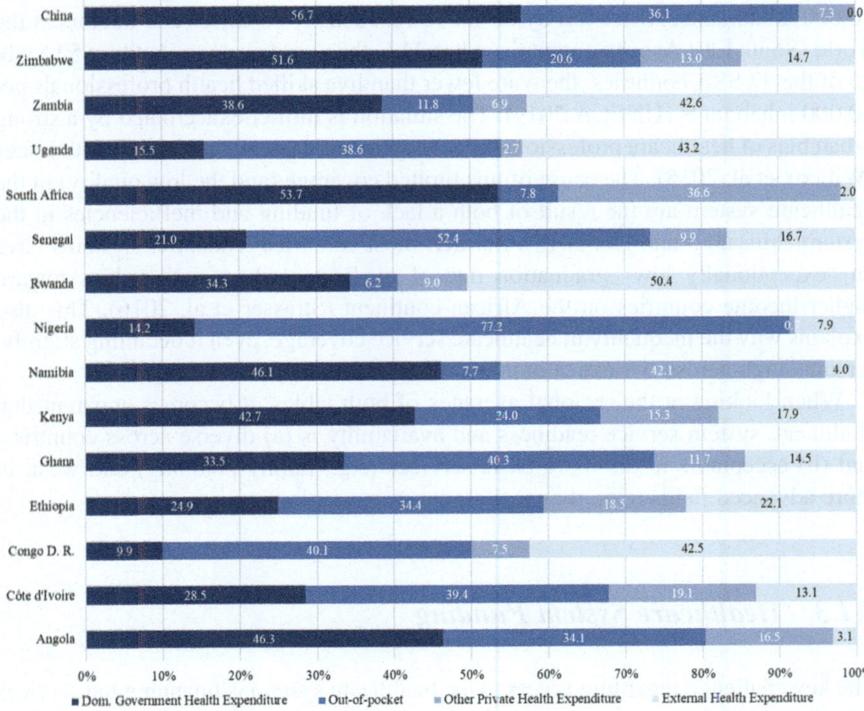

Fig. 5.1 Sources of healthcare funding as % of total health expenditure 2017. Source: WHO (n.d.)

increased the share of government funding between 2000 and 2017, sometimes significantly, as in Tanzania (21 percentage points), South Africa (17 percentage points), Rwanda (16 percentage points), and Kenya (14 percentage points). Compared to China (nearly 35 percentage points) the development is, however, somewhat slow. These SSA countries seem to be moving toward better, if not universal, healthcare coverage. In order to achieve Universal Health Coverage, there is no alternative to general public tax-based spending as the main source of finance. However, the current situation is low per capita public healthcare spending which is stalling despite rising shares in healthcare spending as a percentage of total government spending. The reasons are (a) the low government revenue base since tax collection systems are usually underdeveloped in African economies and (b) population growth (World Bank 2016). Attempts to improve healthcare services with existing per capita spending on healthcare levels are in the field of strategic public procurement and increasing efficiency in the healthcare system (Willcox et al. 2015). The countries that have experienced a declining share of government funding tend to have rising out-of-pocket spending, e.g., Nigeria saw a decline in government funding of 4.1 percentage points and an increase in out-of-pocket spending of 17.1 percentage points between 2000 and 2017. In Angola and Uganda, a similar effect can be observed only that the compensation for declining public funding is by external funds (WHO n.d.; World Bank 2016).

The second most important source of healthcare funding is out-of-pocket spending, which accounts for more than 36.7% of total healthcare spending in all of SSA, a 4.3 percentage point increase between 2000 and 2016 (WHO 2018). The out-of-pocket-spending shares between 2000 and 2017 declined in 34 of the 45 SSA countries with data.[2] Of these, 22 countries had a declining spending level that was double-digit; only 11 countries showed rising out-of-pocket spending as a share of total healthcare expenditure. However, 25% of the SSA countries have an out-of-pocket spending share of more than 50% of total healthcare spending (20 countries with more than 40% of total healthcare spending). To date the share of out-of-pocket spending in total healthcare expenditure remains very high and differs substantially across countries: It ranged from 3% (Botswana) to 77% (Nigeria) in 2017. Looking at the absolute value per person of annual out-of-pocket spending on healthcare in SSA over the years, it has nearly doubled from USD39 (PPP) in 2000 to USD72.6 in 2016. The range across countries is big: In 2017 the country with the lowest per capita out-of-pocket spending on healthcare was Mozambique with USD4.6 (PPP) p.a. while Mauritius had the highest with USD624 (PPP) p.a. (WHO n.d.; World Bank n.d.-b). A country focus on out-of-pocket spending to finance healthcare is problematic in terms of poverty (Kutzin et al. 2016). The World Bank (2016) has estimated that approximately 11 million people in Africa slipped into poverty due to out-of-pocket spending on healthcare. The share of out-of-pocket spending in total private spending is much higher for poor households than for rich ones. This aggravates poverty issues in the countries (Musango and Ota 2015; WHO 2017b). The high share of out-of-pocket spending creates a barrier to accessing health services especially for the BoP (UNECA 2019).

> The poor suffer disproportionately from the burden of ill-health. Investment in health is therefore pro-poor, as well as enabling a productive workforce to boost growth. The risk of future pandemics in Africa makes scaling up support to regional health systems a major priority. (AfDB et al. 2017)

This quote indicates the relevance of finding ways of reaching the Bottom of the Pyramid with health services and pharmaceuticals so that the productivity loss and other indirect negative economic effects are mitigated.

The third method of funding healthcare and providing services is via international non-governmental organizations (NGOs) or multilateral organizations such as the World Bank. The role of external funding varies significantly between countries: In countries like South Africa (2%), Angola (3.1%), and Namibia (4%) the share of external financial support for healthcare provision is low. By contrast, Rwanda (50.4%), Uganda (43.6%), Zambia (42.6%), and Democratic Republic of Congo (32.5%) have a high dependency on external funding (WHO n.d.). These sources of funding are not considered sustainable and are often linked to other political topics

[2]This decline in out-of-pocket spending mainly occurred in smaller countries and was, on a regional level, overcompensated by high out-of-pocket spending increases in large countries such as Nigeria.

(The Economist 2017b). The share of *Development Assistance for Health* (DAH) funding in the low-income countries of Africa rose from 20% of total health spending in 2000 to 35% in 2014. This increase was mainly driven by HIV, followed by spending on fighting malaria (World Bank 2016). Strasser et al. (2016) see this targeted approach of external healthcare aid as insufficient to ensure a comprehensive and sustainable coverage of the population's needs.

The final source of financing healthcare services falls under "other voluntary funding schemes."[3] The role of such schemes is relatively low, with the exception of South Africa and Namibia, indicating that there is a private insurance market remaining to be developed in most countries (WHO n.d.). The important role of individual activities to ensure funding for health services has led to the rise of innovative concepts. Mobile phones and basic digital technology are used in an attempt to spread healthcare coverage to the poor population. Lee et al. (2017) found some 487 mHealth programs across all Sub-Saharan African countries with a strong cluster in East Africa. They point out that high mobile phone penetration and reliable infrastructure is a pre-requirement for mHealth solutions, factors that are not present in all countries. One example of an innovative mHealth insurance scheme is M-TIBA in Kenya.[4] Citizens can sign up for a mobile health wallet and can add any dependent family member they want to have access to primary healthcare. It works like a healthcare savings account where the funds can be used to pay for outpatient healthcare services and medication in any of over 400 health facilities across Kenya (M-TIBA n.d.). The advantage for healthcare providers is more customers with available funds to pay for treatment and drugs. On a wider scale, however, Strasser et al. (2016) point out that there is a rampant lack of eHealth strategies among the African countries.

In summary, the current structure of healthcare system funding does not ensure continuous accessibility to, and readiness of, healthcare services for the population. The reasons are the lack of public healthcare provision and a strong reliance on out-of-pocket spending, which places a strain on private household budgets, especially for the poor. In addition, a gradually declining share of external funding of healthcare expenditures (esp. NGOs) can be observed. High out-of-pocket spending also explains the high price sensitivity. This is the challenge that multinational pharmaceutical companies face when attempting to target the BoP market in Sub-Saharan Africa.

---

[3]This includes private insurance, enterprise and NGO-based insurance schemes, and voluntary insurance models.

[4]M-Tiba is the first of a series of similar schemes in Sub-Saharan African countries offering similar healthcare schemes all based on the Pharma Access Foundation concept (https://www.pharmaccess.org/) run by CarePay, a legal entity founded in Kenya.

5.2 Pharmaceutical Market in Sub-Saharan Africa

Access to medicine is one key target of the African Health Strategy (AHS) and of Universal Health Coverage. This chapter will provide an overview of the pharmaceutical market in Sub-Saharan Africa by assessing supply and demand-side key data in 2014 for important countries provided in Table 5.3.

5.2.1 Demand

The market for medicine products in (all of) Africa is rather limited but has exhibited strong growth for the past 15 years. It grew from USD4.7 bn in 2003 to USD20.8 bn in 2016.[5] It is expected to reach USD40 bn by 2020. The generics segment alone has grown by 9% p.a. since 2013 (Lartey et al. 2018). The market for only SSA was estimated at USD14 bn in 2017. For comparison: India and China, countries with similar populations as Africa, have market sizes of USD19 bn and USD124 bn, respectively. The per capita sales of pharmaceuticals are largely similar. The average for the countries in the table stands at USD20.1 (Germany has USD667.1) with a huge variety in values ranging from under USD5 (Dem. Rep. of Congo, Ethiopia) to USD68 (South Africa) and USD82 (Namibia). Spending on pharmaceuticals accounts for a large proportion of total health spending, on average 22% going up as much as 42% (Burkina Faso) and as low as 5% (Nigeria).

Most of the market is supplied through imports, which are estimated to account for 70–90% of total demand, depending on the country. Imports of medicine in 2018 was some USD9.9 billion, more or less evenly split across the regions with the exception of Central Africa. The long-term growth stood at 12.4% in SSA slowing down to 4.6% in the medium-term which was, except for Southern Africa, above 5% p.a. in all regions, led by East Africa with 6.4% (UNCTAD n.d.). These high growth rates can be attributed to the acknowledgment of governments that health is a key contributor to economic growth and is the result of the increasing efforts to create universal healthcare coverage (compare Sect. 5.1). It is also the result of a lack of a notable local pharmaceutical industry (see next section).

The most attractive markets are in the urban regions as opposed to rural areas which is in line with the distribution of wealth and poverty within a country (Conway et al. 2019). Despite the growth rates, the availability of medicine among the population is limited. The availability of a set of selected generic medicines in a sample of Sub-Saharan African countries remains between 21% (Congo) and 88% (Mauritius) of the population (see Table 5.1). Large differences between countries and outlets (private vs. public) can be observed (WHO 2017a).

[5]To avoid confusion, the market size in Table 5.3 refers to only countries in Sub-Saharan Africa. North Africa makes up a large proportion of any industry market in Africa.

Table 5.3 Pharmaceutical industry KPIs in selected SSA countries 2014

	Number of employees	Gross VA in m USD	Labor productivity[a] (Proxy)	Exports in m USD	Imports in m USD	Trade balance in m USD	Market size[b] in m USD	Total sales in m USD	Total sales USD per Capita	Pharma sales as % of HC expenditure
Angola	6552	137.8	21,032	n.d.	239.2	n.d.	n.d.	330	13.5	7.5
Burkina Faso	1037	19.2	18,515	n.d.	190.3	n.d.	n.d.	260	14.9	42.3
Cameroon	5242	95.8	18,275	0.6	234.9	−234.3	330.1	370	16.1	27.4
Congo, Dem. Rep.	977	125.3	No calc.	n.d.	79.4	n.d.	n.d.	360	4.7	30.0
Côte d'Ivoire	5048	103.0	20,404	5.2	375.9	−370.7	473.7	490	22.3	25.2
Ethiopia	660	27.0	40,909	2.0	309.8	−307.8	334.8	460	4.7	17.6
Ghana	3490	45.9	13,152	1.4	206.2	−204.8	250.7	330	12.3	25.0
Kenya	3505	74.8	21,341	87.0	475.5	−388.5	463.3	730	16.2	20.8
Mozambique	1467	18.6	12,679	0.6	164.4	−163.8	182.4	240	8.9	21.2
Namibia	1846	30.6	16,576	1.2	152.6	−151.4	182.0	200	82.2	16.5
Nigeria	7780	1244.0	No calc.	8.0	314.5	−306.5	1550.5	1030	5.8	5.2
Rwanda	309	4.7	15,210	0.1	94.6	−94.5	99.2	130	11.5	22.0
Senegal	3855	44.1	11,440	13.8	193.5	−179.7	223.8	310	20.9	42.3
South Africa	97,000	946.5	9758	380.0	1901.7	−1521.7	2468.2	3670	68	11.9
Tanzania	1600	61.0	38,125	2.8	310.9	−308.1	369.1	480	9.3	18.0
Uganda	1260	31.0	24,603	9.9	354.4	−344.5	375.5	430	11.5	22.3
Zambia	1460	25.0	17,123	0.1	208.2	−208.1	233.1	240	15.3	17.9
Zimbabwe	676	19.0	28,107	2.2	246.7	−244.5	263.5	360	23.7	n.a.
Total or average of selected SSA countries	**143,764**	**3053.3**	**21,238.3**	**515**	**6053**	**−5537.8**	**8591.1**	**9470**	**20.1**	**21.9**

Source: IFPMA (2017); own calculations
[a]Calculated as: Labor Productivity = GVA/no of workers
[b]Calculated as: Market size = GVA + Imports − Exports
VA value added, *HC* healthcare, *No calc.* no KPI calculated as data is inconsistent

5.2.2 *Production*

Looking at production in more detail, the industry is relatively small with only an estimated 375 drug manufacturers in Africa (China has approximately 5000 producers and India 10,500). The pharmaceutical manufacturers in SSA are concentrated in 9 of the 46 countries. The biggest manufacturing countries, accounting for 72% of all SSA producers, are Nigeria (128 companies), South Africa (68), Kenya (42), and Ghana (32) (Lartey et al. 2018). In most cases, the manufacturers import active pharmaceutical ingredients and then locally formulate the medicine. Up to 100 SSA manufacturers limit their activities to (re-)packaging. In terms of market reach, local producers limit their activities to local markets because of a lack of modern facilities, equipment, analytical instruments, and experienced human capital. These aspects result in low labor productivity: Most SSA countries boast between USD10,000 and USD40,000 output value per worker. By way of comparison, Germany has a productivity of USD204,000 per worker (IFPMA 2017). Only three companies in SSA—two in South Africa, one in Ghana—produce active pharma ingredients without engaging in their own research and development (Conway et al. 2019). Thus, the domestic pharmaceutical industry can be said to be in a nascent state and typically not competitive internationally (Lartey et al. 2018). It was calculated by Conway et al. (2019) that a drug's landed cost from India into Ethiopia and Nigeria would be 5–15% more expensive than local production. This is in spite of the need to import all the ingredients for drug manufacture. Because of the lower import tariffs for intermediate products and the lower cost of entering the local distribution system for local producers, they can exist in the (protected) markets. The authors, however, find this scenario to be unlikely for all other countries investigated due to the lower capacity and utilization rates compared to India. Thus, the small country market size plays a critical role in the lack of competitiveness of SSA pharmaceutical production as no economies of scale can be used.

As a response to this lack of local pharmaceutical production and high dependence on imports the *Pharmaceutical Manufacturing Plan for Africa (PMPA)* was initiated in Accra in 2007 and finalized in Addis Ababa in 2012, where a business plan for the implementation was signed by the heads of state. The objective is to support the creation and strengthening of a local African manufacturing base for pharmaceuticals (African Union 2015). The motives to focus on the pharmaceutical industry are (1) guaranteeing access to medicine as part of the Universal Health Coverage plans of governments (compare the previous chapter), (2) technology transfer, and (3) job creation well beyond the pharmaceutical industry (Lartey et al. 2018). The Business Plan for the implementation of the PMPA points out existing challenges for setting up pharmaceutical production in Sub-Saharan Africa thus explaining the current situation of little local, indigenous production:

1. There is a lack of local Active Pharma Ingredients in Africa. They account for some 60% of total medicine value-added and it is estimated, for the total of Africa, that 95% are imported (African Union 2012).

2. There is a lack of quality and standards in the production of drugs. "Problems related to quality, price and red tape leave consumers short-changed and local manufacturers struggling to compete with large-scale foreign producers, particularly from China and India" (Pearson and Milimo 2017).
3. There is an insufficient regulatory system to facilitate and control pharmaceutical production (African Union 2012).
4. There is a shortage of skilled scientists and know-how in SSA countries.
5. On their own, most African markets are too small to allow for any type of local production going beyond formulation and packaging as there is no scope for economics of scale (Pearson and Milimo 2017).

Lartey et al. (2018) see some progress being made with the implementation of the PMPA, especially with regard to regulations and institutions to facilitate building up manufacturing capacities. A key achievement of the implementation plan so far has been the set-up of the *African Medicines Regulatory Harmonization* program. It aims to simplify processes and to harmonize regulatory rules across countries and, thus, reduce registration cost and time by aligning registration requirements across Africa. This would make it easier for pharmaceutical companies to address a large enough market. The effectiveness of these institutions still needs to be proven.

5.2.3 Distribution

Studies show that logistics to and within Africa are expensive and unreliable (see study on West Africa by Carlowitz and Röndigs 2016). This is why international companies tend to use local distributors (or international distributors with a strong African footprint) to bring their products to the African markets. Therefore, for international pharmaceutical companies, the key success factor in their African business is to find a suitable, reliable, and compliant distributor. Usually multinational pharmaceutical manufacturers export fob (free on board) from the international harbor to the receiving African port. On occasions, they export directly to government institutions (tender business) where the volumes are large (and prices low). However, even then delivery is usually fob.

The World Health Organization investigated distribution costs for medicines in SSA and found a range of mark-ups of factors from 2 to 14 on top of the producer's price.[6] They interestingly also show that the mark-up is (significantly) higher for prices sold to private customers as opposed to public customers (WHO 2017a). The main challenges for countries to guarantee access to medicine, especially for the BoP, are:

[6]They calculate the factor according to following formula: factor = local price/international reference price.

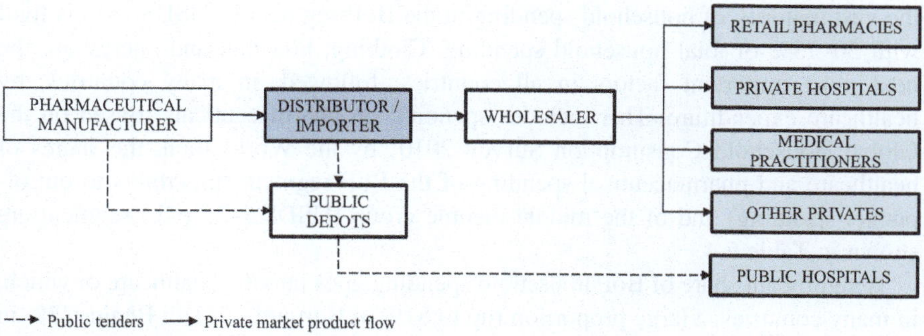

Fig. 5.2 Standard distribution model of the pharmaceutical industry in Africa. Source: Based on Camelot Management Consultants (2017)

> Long lead times in international procurement, fragile logistics and storage capacity, and high transport and distribution costs hinder the broad access and affordability of essential medicines. (Dong and Mirza 2016)

This is supported by statements on improving distribution in order to reduce the costs of supplying medicine, thus making it more affordable for consumers and more profitable for companies (Camelot Management Consultants 2017).

The structure of distribution—that is value delivery—in the African drug markets is organized as shown in Fig. 5.2.

The distribution logic varies from country to country depending on the availability of qualified wholesalers. Very often the distributor/importer functions as the wholesaler. Nigeria has some 724 licensed distributors. In other countries, out-patient clinics act as key distribution points for drugs at the retail level. One Kenyan out-patient clinic generated up to 70% of its turnover via its integrated pharmacy department (Zekeng 2016). In terms of pharmacy chains, there has been a wave of consolidation, often driven by South African retailers such as Clicks or Shoprite (supermarket) (Holt et al. 2015). However, consolidation is still on a small scale compared to other countries. For instance, in Kenya, the largest pharmacy chain (owned by a South African retailer) is Goodlife Pharmacy with 47 stores followed by Halton with 20 pharmacies (Adegoke 2019).

5.2.4 *Pharmaceutical Spending in the BoP*

The analysis so far has been on the overall pharmaceutical market without reference to the BoP. The first question is how much do they spend on healthcare and on pharmaceuticals as a share of their total household spending?[7] In all SSA countries,

[7]Note that this refers to 'household spending' which corresponds only to the out-of-pocket healthcare spending and does not reflect total healthcare spending in the country.

the vast majority of household spending in the BoP segment (<USD3 p.d.) is food with 50–75% of total household spending. Clothing, housing, and energy are the next most important factors in all countries, followed, in many countries, by healthcare expenditure. This includes spending on pharmaceuticals. Based on the Global Household Consumption Survey 2010[8] by the World Bank the shares of healthcare and pharmaceutical spending of the BoP segment (this refers to out-of-pocket spending) and of the middle-income group (USD8.5–23 p.d.) segment are shown in Table 5.4.

A significant share of BoP household spending goes into the healthcare of which, in many countries, a large proportion (up to 81% in Burundi, 79% in Benin, 77% in Senegal, 72% in Togo) is on pharmaceuticals. At the other end of the range, Tanzania spends only 9% of its healthcare spending on pharmaceuticals. There are some other countries with low shares of pharmaceuticals in healthcare spending. This might be due to better coverage of healthcare insurance (as in Kenya) which reduces out-of-pocket-spending on healthcare and pharmaceuticals, in particular. Interestingly the share of healthcare and medicine spending is similar across the two income groups for many countries. This is slightly counter-intuitive as one would expect the share of spending on basic requirements to decline with rising income. This is not the case for all SSA countries for two reasons: One, the income level for middle-income is still not excessively high meaning that not everyone engages in healthcare insurance cover but rather opts for out-of-pocket-spending. Two, in many countries there is no alternative to out-of-pocket-spending as no insurance system exists.

More detailed information about the BoP potential for pharmaceutical companies can be obtained by looking at the sales potential of the pharmaceutical market in the BoP segment. The main question is how to tap the large rural market, which accounts for 46% of total household spending on medicines (2010) in Africa (World Bank n. d.-a). In rural areas access to medicine is harder, purchasing power is low, and the reach of the healthcare system is limited. Yet if Universal Health Coverage is to be achieved this segment has to be accessed. The relevance of the discussion on the Bottom of the Pyramid market segment is revealed by looking at the 2010 Global Household Consumption data in Table 5.5.

In most countries, more than 50% of national pharmaceutical demand lies with the BoP. In urban areas, where the BoP are more easily reached, the share of BoP expenditure on medicines is—despite large slum populations—significantly lower. This indicates the concentration of high and middle-income groups in cities. Among the countries with relatively large urban markets are Côte d'Ivoire, Cameron, Democratic Republic of Congo, and Nigeria. These are interesting BoP markets for two reasons: (1) They are relatively easy to access compared to the rural BoP customers, and (2) the urban BoP per capita healthcare spending is higher. However, in all countries the pharmaceutical market size of the BoP segment in rural regions is (much) higher than that in urban areas. In most countries in 2010 the share of BoP

[8]More current data is not available.

Table 5.4 Household spending on healthcare and drugs: BoP versus middle income 2010[a]

	BoP segment—National level(<USD3 p.d.)			Middle income segment—National level(USD8.5 and USD23 p.d.)		
	Share of health spending in total consumption(in %)	Share of pharma spending in total consumption(in %)	Share of pharma in health spending (in %)	Share of health spending in total consumption (in %)	Share of pharma spending in total consumption (in %)	Share of pharma in health spending (in %)
Benin	5.1	4.0	78.9	4.6	3.4	75.3
Burkina Faso	2.1	0.9	43.2	2.9	0.7	25.6
Burundi	5.2	4.3	81.4	4.7	3.9	82.7
Cameroon	4.7	3.2	69.1	3.4	1.8	53.9
Congo, Dem. Rep.	2.6	0.9	35.5	0.6	0.4	70.0
Côte d'Ivoire	4.8	2.9	60.0	3.8	2.3	59.3
Ethiopia	0.4	0.2	44.2	0.6	0.2	43.3
Ghana	1.7	1.0	62.3	1.2	0.7	60.2
Kenya	2.2	0.8	34.5	2.6	0.4	15.3
Mozambique	0.5	0.2	32.2	1.2	0.3	24.5
Namibia	1.0	0.2	20.1	2.1	0.4	20.1
Nigeria	9.2	4.2	45.3	20.3	9.2	45.6
Rwanda	1.9	0.4	20.3	1.2	0.1	9.1
Senegal	2.3	1.8	77.1	2.4	1.4	56.0
South Africa	1.5	0.9	56.9	1.1	0.6	56.5
Tanzania	1.5	0.1	9.1	0.7	0.0	6.4
Togo	4.5	3.2	71.9	3.4	2.5	73.1
Uganda	6.0	3.7	62.3	4.0	2.6	64.6
Zambia	0.2	0.1	22.4	0.3	0.0	12.9

Sources: World Bank (n.d.-a)

[a]The middle-income segment was selected for two reasons: (1) the data availability for the high-income group was sketchy, and (2) the middle class would be the first income segment with sufficient income levels as to go beyond subsistence spending patterns

Table 5.5 National versus urban household spending on drugs by BoP segment 2010[a]

	BoP—Household consumption of pharmaceutical products 2010					
	National			Urban		
	BoP spending as % of total pharma market	BoP spending (in m USD)	Per capita spending p.a. by BoP-segment[b] in USD	BoP spending as % of total pharma market	BoP spending (in m USD)	Per capita spending p.a. by BoP segment[b] in USD
Benin	74.9	96.3	11.9	61.7	43.5	13.2
Burkina Faso	76.9	30.3	2.0	58.8	11.7	3.5
Burundi	92.7	54.7	6.7	66.4	7.3	10.1
Cameroon	60.6	164.4	10.4	44.2	80.2	12.4
Congo, D. R.	97.0	127.5	2.0	93.6	51.0	2.3
Cote d'Ivoire	33.5	157.8	13.2	19.9	58.4	13.6
Ethiopia	45.6	34.0	0.6	30.4	8.3	1.2
Ghana	34.0	55.0	3.8	19.4	19.5	4.0
Kenya	59.8	89.5	2.6	30.8	18.4	3.6
Mozambique	62.0	6.8	0.3	46.3	3.4	0.6
Namibia	15.0	1.5	0.9	7.5	0.6	1.3
Nigeria	55.8	2180.3	15.4	48.2	935.1	14.2
Rwanda	69.3	6.6	0.7	42.4	2.0	1.7
Senegal	53.2	65.7	6.8	33.2	25.4	8.9
South Africa	10.4	96.8	4.9	5.6	44.2	5.5
Tanzania	85.2	11.4	0.3	74.4	5.3	0.5
Togo	69.8	50.1	9.3	51.2	20.4	12.2
Uganda	59.8	278.9	10.0	20.5	23.4	9.5
Zambia	70.5	1.9	0.2	56.5	1.0	0.2

Sources: World Bank (n.d.-a)

[a]Interpreting the percentage-values one needs to understand how they are calculated: Spending on medical products *by lowest income group (BoP)* (<USD3 p.d.) divided by total spending on medical products *across all income groups*. It shows the relevance of the BoP segment in the demand for pharmaceutical products in African countries

[b]<USD3 p.d.

spending on drugs (as a percentage of total drug spending in the country) was highest in rural areas because the relative size of the BoP population segment is large. Thus, it is in these areas that the share of BoP consumption of the country's total pharmaceutical market can exceed 90% in countries such as the Democratic Republic of Congo (99%), Burundi (95%), Rwanda (97%), and Tanzania (98%). Hence, if companies want to have a wide reach and ensure large volumes it is hard to ignore the BoP in rural areas despite the significant distribution challenges. However, on the one hand, the absolute figures should not be used as market sizes as they are not up to date. This is because no new survey has been conducted since 2010. On the other hand, the overall tendency seems to be the same since a study of more current indicators leads to similar conclusions.

The analysis of household spending on pharmaceutical data (which is out-of-pocket-spending) allows for three clear statements:

1. In most Sub-Saharan African countries the highest proportion of out-of-pocket (household) spending on pharmaceuticals is from the lowest income group (<USD3 per day) going up to 93% of total spending on pharmaceuticals at the national level.
2. The majority of pharmaceutical consumption (in USD million) is by poor households in rural areas. Their share of total national drug spending can reach 99%. This implies that the Bottom of the Pyramid segment for pharmaceuticals is most pronounced in rural areas across SSA. This rural location causes logistical and distribution challenges when pharmaceutical companies try to address that segment.
3. Per capita purchasing power on pharmaceuticals is significantly higher in urban areas.

5.3 Conclusion

The types and structures of healthcare systems in African countries differ widely. Some commonalities can be discerned, however: Most countries try to implement some sort of Universal Health Coverage to be driven mainly by public funding. However, most countries do not manage to provide sufficient government funding for healthcare spending owing to a low tax base, low efficiency in their healthcare systems, and rapid population growth. The result is a high/rising share of out-of-pocket spending on healthcare in most of the countries, even becoming a source of poverty in several countries. Significant inequality between the poorer population segments and the wealthier segment remains in terms of access and quality of healthcare coverage, making the provision of healthcare services to the poor a key concern for the development of countries. Observing the household consumption pattern, it is safe to state that the market volume in pharmaceuticals of the BoP market segment plays a significant role in Sub-Saharan Africa, both in (hard to reach) rural areas and urban areas.

It is important to find new ways of how to provide Bottom of the Pyramid market segments with healthcare services and with pharmaceutical products. On the one hand, the larger BoP markets in absolute terms lie in rural areas while, on the other, BoP per capita spending is higher in urban areas.

References

Adegoke Y (2019) Ghanaian startup mPharma is buying Kenya's second largest pharmacy chain. Quartz Africa, March 28, 2019. https://qz.com/africa/1582487/ghanas-mpharma-buys-kenya-pharmacy-haltons/. Accessed 3 Feb 2020

AfDB, OECD, UNDP (2017) African Economic Outlook 2017. OECD, Paris

African Union (2012) Pharmaceutical manufacturing plan for Africa – business plan. Addis Abeba

African Union (2015) Update on implementation of the pharmaceutical manufacturing plan for Africa (PMPA). First Meeting of the Specialised Technical Committee on Health, Population and Drug Control 13-15.4.2015. Addis Abeba. http://carmma.org/resource/report-first-meeting-specialised-technical-committee-health-population-and-drug-control. Accessed 17 Feb 2019

African Union (2016) Africa Health Strategy 2016-2030. https://au.int/en/documents/30357/africa-health-strategy-2016-2030. Accessed 23 Nov 2019

Afrobarometer (n.d.) The online data analysis tool (R7 2016/2018). http://afrobarometer.org/online-data-analysis/analyse-online. Accessed 24 Jan 2018

Armah-Attoh D, Selormey E, Houessou R (2016) Despite gains, barriers keep health care high on Africa's priority list. Afrobarometer Policy Paper 31. https://afrobarometer.org/sites/default/files/publications/Policy%20papers/ab_r6_policypaperno31_health_a_priority_in_africa1.pdf. Accessed 18 Sept 2019

Camelot Management Consultants (2017) Navigating the labyrinth of pharma distribution in Africa. A blueprint to network optimization. https://www.camelot-mc.com/de/study/navigating-the-labyrinth-of-pharma-distribution-in-africa/. Accessed 9 Jul 2020

Cameron E, Nuzzo J, Bell J (2019) Global Health Security Index 2019: Report and model. https://www.ghsindex.org/report-model/. Accessed 15 Apr 2020

Conway M, Holt T, Sabow A, Sun I (2019) Should sub-Saharan Africa make its own drugs? Public Sector Practice, McKinsey & Company. https://www.mckinsey.com/industries/public-sector/our-insights/should-sub-saharan-africa-make-its-own-drugs. Accessed 20 Apr 2020

Dong J, Mirza Z (2016) Supporting the production of pharmaceuticals in Africa. Bull World Health Organ 94:71–72

EY (2018) Global analysis of health insurance in Sub-Saharan Africa. https://www.ey.com/Publication/vwLUAssets/EY-global-analysis-of-health-insurance-in-sub-saharan-africa/%24File/ey-global-analysis-of-health-insurance-in-sub-saharan-africa.pdf. Accessed 12 Feb 2020

Gebre-Mariam T, Tahir K, Gebre-Amanuel S (2016) Bringing industrial and health policies closer: reviving pharmaceutical production in Ethiopia. In: Mackintosh M, Banda G, Tibandebage P, Wamae W (eds) Making medicines in Africa: the political economy of industrializing for local health. Palgrave Macmillan UK, London, pp 65–84

Holt T, Lahrichi M, Santos da Silva J (2015) Africa: a continent of opportunity for pharma and patients. https://www.mckinsey.com/industries/pharmaceuticals-and-medical-products/our-insights/africa-a-continent-of-opportunity-for-pharma-and-patients. Accessed 15 Jul 2018

IFPMA (2017) The pharmaceutical industry and global health. Facts and Figures 2017. Geneva. https://www.ifpma.org/resource-centre/ifpma-facts-and-figures-report/. Accessed 18 Nov 2019

Kutzin J, Yip W, Cashin C (2016) Alternative financing strategies for universal health coverage. In: Scheffler R (ed) World Scientific Handbook of Global Health Economics and Public Policy. Imperial College Press, London, pp 267–309

Lartey PA, Graham AE, Lukulay PH, Ndomondo-Sigonda M (2018) Pharmaceutical sector development in Africa: progress to date. Pharm Med 32:1–11

Lee S, Cho Y-M, Kim S-Y (2017) Mapping mHealth (mobile health) and mobile penetrations in sub-Saharan Africa for strategic regional collaboration in mHealth scale-up: an application of exploratory spatial data analysis. Glob Health 13:63ff

Mackintosh M, Mugwagwa J, Banda G, Tibandebage P, Tunguhole J, Wangwe S, Karimi Njeru M (2018) Health-industry linkages for local health: reframing policies for African health system strengthening. Health Policy Plan 33:602–610

Mohandas B (2019) Healthcare in Africa: reflections on a decade of transformation. Private Healthc Emerg Markets 7:3–6

M-TIBA (n.d.) About us. http://pharmaccess.m-tiba.org/about. Accessed 25 June 2018

Musango L, Ota M (2015) The critical role of health financing in progressing universal health coverage. The African Health Monitor. Special Issue: Universal Health Coverage 20:3–10

Pearson B, Milimo E (2017) Africa's pharmaceutical futures. Afr Rep 91:68–69. https://www.theafricareport.com/802/africas-pharmaceutical-futures/. Accessed 18 Mar 2018

Russo G, Banda G (2015) Re-thinking pharmaceutical production in Africa; Insights from the analysis of the local manufacturing dynamics in Mozambique and Zimbabwe. Stud Comp Int Dev 50:258–281

Strasser R, Kam SM, Regalado SM (2016) Rural health care access and policy in developing countries. Annu Rev Public Health 37:395–412

The Economist (2017a) Access to healthcare in Africa and the Middle East. Economist Intelligence Unit, London

The Economist (2017b) Access to healthcare. Building sustainable health systems. Economist Intelligence Unit, London

UN (2015) Transforming our world: the 2030 agenda for sustainable development. United Nations, New York

UNCTAD (n.d.) Statistical Database. https://unctadstat.unctad.org/EN/. Accessed 23 Feb 2020

UNECA (2019) Economic report on Africa 2019: Fiscal policy for financing sustainable development in Africa. Economic Commission for Africa. Addis Ababa

von Carlowitz P, Röndigs A (2016) Distribution in Afrika. Distributionslogistik in Westafrika als Beispiel. Springer Gabler, Wiesbaden

WHO (2017a) Atlas of the African Health Statistics 2017. WHO Regional Office for Africa. Brazzaville

WHO (2017b) World Health Statistics 2017. Monitoring health for the SDGs. Sustainable development goals. Geneva

WHO (2018) Atlas of African health statistics 2018: Universal health coverage and the sustainable development goals in the WHO African Region. Brazzaville

WHO (n.d.) Global Health Expenditure Database. http://apps.who.int/nha/database. Accessed 16 Apr 2020

Willcox ML, Peersman W, Daou P, Diakité C, Bajunirwe F, Mubangizi V, Mahmoud EH, Moosa S, Phaladze N, Nkomazana O, Khogali M, Diallo D, Maeseneer J de, Mant D (2015) Human resources for primary health care in sub-Saharan Africa: progress or stagnation? Human Resource Health 13:76ff

World Bank (2016) UHC in Africa: a framework for action. Washington, DC. https://openknowledge.worldbank.org/handle/10986/26072. Accessed 18 Jun 2019

World Bank (n.d.-a) Global Consumption Database. http://datatopics.worldbank.org/consumption/home. Accessed 15 Feb 2018

World Bank (n.d.-b) World Development Indicator Database. https://data.worldbank.org/products/wdi. Accessed 4 Aug 2018

Zekeng E (2016) Healthcare systems in Sub-Saharan Africa: focusing on community-based delivery (CBD) of health services and the development of local research institutes. United Nations Peace Progr 3:44–49

Chapter 6
Pharmaceutical MNCs Addressing the BoP Market: Empirical Analysis

The previous chapters provided insights into the theoretical foundations of the BoP concept, the business model approach, and the situation in Sub-Saharan Africa before turning to an overview of the healthcare system and the pharmaceutical market, always with an eye on the role of the BoP. The aim of this chapter is to consolidate all those insights and to move the investigation to the empirical level.

This chapter is based on interviews with experts from multinational pharmaceutical companies that are active in addressing the BoP customer segment in Sub-Saharan Africa. It follows the logic of business model development as discussed in Chap. 3. The aim is to identify key components of successful business models in the pharmaceutical industry with a focus on BoP customers in SSA. For the development of a new business model, it is very important to integrate industry-specific insights and engage practitioners, in this case, successful MNCs in the pharmaceutical sector that operate in BoP markets in SSA. The research question, therefore, can be specified:

> How do profitable business models of multinational pharmaceutical companies that target the BoP in Sub-Saharan Africa have to be designed regarding value proposition, value generation, value capture/revenue model, and the network of partners?

This chapter addresses one of the mentioned research gaps in literature (see Chap. 3). It intends to empirically investigate how profitable business models of multinational pharmaceutical companies targeting the BoP in SSA have to be set up. With this empirical analysis, this book contributes to the understanding of business model design to successfully address the BoP in Sub-Saharan Africa.

This chapter begins with a brief methodological overview to introduce the empirical analysis followed by the results of the analysis and a discussion with recommendations.

P. von Carlowitz, *Success in the Bottom of the Pyramid Market in Africa*,
SpringerBriefs in Business, https://doi.org/10.1007/978-3-030-59068-0_6

6.1 Methodology of Empirical Analysis

This study makes use of the methods of empirical social research which can be defined as "systematic recording and interpretation of social phenomena" (Atteslander 2000). Given the relatively unexplored nature of the BoP business models of multinational pharmaceutical companies in SSA, this study adopts an exploratory qualitative research approach, focusing on companies with successful operations in the BoP in SSA.

Semi-structured expert interviews are chosen in which the interviewer asks about a topic following a manual of guiding questions (Garz and Kraimer 1991; Kromrey 1998; Saunders et al. 2012). There are no pre-fabricated answers so that experts can freely articulate their views. This open approach has the advantage that relevant topics can be discovered which have not yet occurred in the preliminary theoretical considerations. At the same time, the partial standardization ensures the coverage of all topics and allows for comparability on specific topics across interviews. Depending on the course of the interview the interviewer can change question sequences or formulations, delete questions, or ask additional questions (Gläser and Laudel 2006). In this way, the semi-structured expert interview allows a thorough, detailed, and differentiated exploration of all relevant aspects related to the topic (Saunders et al. 2012).

The development of the interview guideline used is theory-driven. Based on the analysis in Chaps. 2 and 3, combined with the insights from Chaps. 4 and 5, core issues for investigation are identified. The goal is to reach a detailed understanding of how precisely a successful business model addressing the BoP segment in SSA needs to be designed from a practical perspective. Then it will be collated to the literature findings. An interview matrix was developed and used to guide the semi-structured interviews and ensure that the relevant topics were covered (Table 6.1).

The relevant population of potential interview partners is drawn from the multi-national pharmaceutical companies with business operations at the BoP in SSA. According to Graneheim and Lundman (2004), the sample must be representative of the universe from which it is drawn. Public statistics were used to identify suitable companies. Companies to include in the study were selected from a list of the 20 largest multinational pharmaceutical companies that are described in the Access to Medicine Index 2016. The Access to Medicine Index analyses how the leading pharmaceutical companies make their products more accessible in BoP markets (Hogerzeil et al. 2016).

The interview partners were selected according to criteria of relevance and knowledge (Garz and Kraimer 1991). In order to be able to make valid statements, senior managers from the selected multinational pharmaceutical firms that lead market access activities in Africa were invited to take part in an interview. They were identified as being best suited to respond to the questions based on their seniority within the company and their experience. In total, five interviews were conducted during February and March 2017. The telephone interviews lasted between 30 and 90 min. All interviewees were asked to approve the use of their

Table 6.1 Development of the interview guideline and link to theory

Section	Situation	Objective	Question
Introduction	Many people in SSA still lack access to medicine because of their limited ability to pay for medicine or they live in rural areas or both	What is the company's presence in the market.	Describe your presence in the SSA BoP market
Value proposition	Not much is known about purchasing or consumer behavior of BoP consumers in SSA	Evaluate product adaptation to meet the needs of the BoP customer	– What products do you offer in SSA? – What is the difference of your product portfolio in SAA compared to other markets? – What value do you provide to BoP customers?
Value generation	– Lack of a healthcare infrastructure negatively affects drug distribution to the BoP – The lack of product awareness and limited understanding of its use are challenges – It is necessary to involve the local community to enable the development of innovative and appropriate solutions	Highlight the way the organization adapts to create, deliver, and capture value?	– How do you produce the products? – How do you promote the products? – How do you ensure the availability of products? – What is the role of the BoP in your value chain? – Is there a difference between how you produce, promote, and distribute products to BoP consumers in SSA compared to other markets? – How do you ensure the ability to scale?
Value capture/revenue model	There is a need to minimize costs	Generate insights into what the revenue model has to look like	– What does your revenue model look like? – Do you make a profit? – How do you manage affordability for the BoP?
Network of partners	It is necessary to collaborate with non-traditional stakeholders such as NGOs and other organizations that already have substantial experience in BoP markets	Evaluate the role and importance of partners in the business model	– Which stakeholders do you collaborate with? – Who are your partners? – How does your collaboration influence the value generation of your products?

Source: Own illustration

data. Full anonymity was guaranteed as is good academic practice. To evaluate the material, all interviews were electronically recorded and transcribed according to the following rules: literal transcription, no dialects, slight smoothing of language, anonymization, and the usage of unique abbreviations for the persons involved (e.g., I = interviewer) (Kuckartz 2010).

Table 6.2 Coding system of the qualitative content analysis

Business model design components	The role and influence of exchange partners	Assessment of the BoP pharma business
Value proposition	Government and public institutions	Importance of BoP business to multinational companies
Value generation	NGOs	Recommendations for implementation
Revenue model	Middlemen/distributors	

Source: Own illustration

The focus of empirical qualitative analysis lies in reducing large information sets to a small set of general statements. This process should result in as little information loss as possible (Graneheim and Lundman 2004). In qualitative research, texts have to be evaluated systematically to obtain reliable data (Cropley 2002). As a method of analysis, the qualitative content analysis according to Mayring (2010) is applied: The transcripts are summarized and then "coded," that is bundled in topical categories (Garz and Kraimer 1991). A simple coding system based on the findings in the literature review and the interview guideline is developed (see Table 6.2).

The analysis of interviews is theory-based, guided by rules, and follows an individual coding system. Thus, the data material retrieved via the interviews is structured according to topical categories and can be systematically analyzed across interviews (Mayring and Gläser-Zikuda 2008). Analysis of the transcribed interviews was done using the software MaxQDA.

6.2 Addressing the Bottom of the Pyramid: Business Model and Success Factors

In the semi-structured interviews, experts were asked about their business operations along the three dimensions of a business model as laid out in Sect. 3.1. The discussion of success factors is based on the insights from the literature as presented in Sect. 3.3. This chapter begins with a general assessment by the expert on their business at the BoP. The analytical part will look at the value proposition and the role of affordability, value generation and the importance of availability and awareness. Next, the value capture dimension in the business model will be investigated. Finally, the role of collaboration, inclusion, and localization which are key for a successful business model in the BoP context, are discussed.

6.2.1 *Business in the BoP Market*

Most experts agree that an engagement in the BoP market is important and a long-term business perspective is needed: "Focusing on the BoP is an investment but if you have a long-term perspective it is worthwhile" (Expert 2). Further, they agree that business models targeting the BoP are linked to social responsibility considerations. However, this is not the dominant reason as is the case in social or inclusive business models. It is rather a complementary effect to the for-profit business approach. During the interviews, the experts described the market and the target group much in line with the literature. Characterizing the BoP consumers, two experts share their definition of who is included in the BoP market. They define people with an annual income between USD1500 and 3000 as belonging to the BoP. The value of USD3000 would slightly exceed the definition of BoP usually found in the literature. Another expert defines BoP customers as having an income of USD700–1500 p.a. which roughly coincides with the BoP definitions in the literature (see Sect. 2.1). Further characteristics of the BoP market segment are high unemployment and a lack of health insurance coverage in most SSA countries. Hence, most of the healthcare spending of the poor population segments is out-of-pocket spending (see Sect. 5.1). This is a drain on the disposable income of the BoP society where the buying behavior can be described as hand-to-mouth as BoP consumers cannot afford to buy weekly or monthly treatment courses of medicine. BoP consumers are typically uninformed about diseases and available treatment and medication:

> Patients are very often not aware of the diseases that they have, and if they do know they often do not know what best to do in order to get the right treatment or how to avoid the diseases. (Expert 1)

In addition, transmitted infections are frequently not communicated to partners. This often includes not returning for treatment. Both aspects contribute to the discrepancy between actual demand and potential demand at the BoP.

Furthermore, access to medicine is limited for large proportions of the BoP segment due to long distances and traveling times. Reaching many BoP communities, especially in rural areas, is difficult. This means it is difficult to supply distribution points such as hospitals, health clinics, or pharmacies. At the same time, patients struggle to reach these distribution points. Geographically the nearest distribution points in rural areas are usually in towns as a result of insufficient logistical infrastructure.

The conditions and characteristics of the BoP customers and market described are in line with the previous chapters. Addressing the BoP requires adjusting to the problems and challenges characterizing this income segment and the specific business environment. If this is not done, then the addressable market will not be sizeable enough and the business model will not be profitable. This brings the analysis to the question as to how the business models account for the specifics of the BoP market.

6.2.2 Value Proposition

A strong value proposition ensures that a company meets the needs of the targeted customer group, here the BoP population, with their offerings, here medicines. Therefore, a company needs to have a detailed understanding of its clients in order to develop a value proposition that helps BoP consumers to fulfill their needs (Gummesson et al. 2010).

When creating a value proposition the business conditions (see Chaps. 4 and 5) with regard to the BoP market segment and the consumers' needs have to feature:

> Just changing the price is not going to solve all the problems of limited access as you go down the wealth pyramid. (Expert 1)

The literature (Anderson 2006) and the experts identified relevant aspects that need to feature in the value proposition for the BoP market segment: affordability, availability, and health awareness.

> It is possible to generate profit in poor areas, [...] but you have to be smart about it and it depends on the product that you need to bring [in]. (Expert 4)

All experts agree that suitable products for BoP customer needs and a very low price to ensure affordability are required: "Selling drugs is about affordability" (Expert 5). According to another expert, products should be relevant, should focus on the diseases most prevalent in the region and should be simple to use. Also, the form of administering should be suited to the consumers' preferences and capabilities. Two of the companies interviewed offer a limited range of generic pharmaceuticals and over-the-counter products with a focus on the most prevalent application fields, i.e., diseases, in the BoP market in SSA. One company specializes in medication for just one disease. These are all levers to raise the volume demanded for the medicine offered. Other companies address the price challenge more directly. One of the companies offers the entire portfolio of generics to the BoP for which no significant R&D costs need to be calculated. In one case, the generic products are licensed to an Indian contract manufacturer to supply the lower-income segments in SSA. The last company takes a pure cost perspective for its portfolio decision and offers medicine for which they are able to sharply reduce the cost or where they are in a niche market with little competition. These different ways of reducing the cost of medicine is not the same as ensuring affordability, as this is all about the producer price and not the consumer price. It is a necessary, but not sufficient, condition for affordability from the BoP consumer perspective.

The majority of experts advocate that a low price need not come with a compromise in quality. They argue that people at the BoP are willing to pay for quality treatment and look at treatment outcomes. This, however, turns out to refer to the upper segments of the BoP income pyramid or the middle-income segments of the population. Simultaneously, lower quality would be "commercial suicide" for multinational drug companies resulting in concerns about their ethical standards (even at the global level). Maintaining quality standards is mainly relevant as the BoP markets are seen as strategically relevant. As income rises, more and higher priced medicines can be sold. Once the market is developed and working it generates higher volumes, which results in economies of scale and lower per-unit costs. As this volume effect occurs in global factories (up to full capacity utilization) it can create higher global profit margins in all countries as a result of the lower cost position and at given prices (see next section).

To summarize, fully in line with the literature's findings, one expert states:

> Access to medicine has different types of dimensions we are talking about: It is about affordability, about the availability of medicine, quality of treatment, but also about awareness. (Expert 5)

How the multinational pharmaceutical companies integrate affordability, availability, quality, health education, and awareness measure into their business model varies and depends on their product portfolio, experience in the market, and corporate strategy. In order for these value propositions to materialize in the BoP segment, there is much strain on the value generation part of the business model. The activities concerning value generation are crucial for the value proposition to become a reality.

6.2.3 Value Generation

Value generation is the part of the business model where the operational activities are organized to allow the value proposition to materialize for the targeted BoP consumer group. Thus, a redesign of the supply chain is important given the specific BoP market conditions. Despite a general agreement among the experts on the value they offer (value proposition), they pursue a variety of different approaches when it comes to value generation. Being successful and capturing value is not just about producer price but also about lowering selling and general administration costs. This is why there are two parts to be discussed with regard to value generation: (1) Sales-related activities and distribution, which refers to value delivery and (2) the production side (value creation).

In order to generate large sales volumes in the BoP market, availability is a main driver. This is the value delivery part of value generation. Experts stress that a business model needs to address access barriers to ensure the availability of medicines for patients. This means offering medicine or health services close to BoP consumers' homes to avoid the obstacle of high travel costs for these poor consumers. This becomes a distribution challenge for pharmaceutical companies. Availability is usually achieved via collaboration with local partners (see below). One company says it has an agreement with Kenyan distributors, some work with the Red Cross and other NGOs, others cooperate with government institutions. The reliability of medicine supply to hospitals, pharmacies, and clinics is an integral part of availability and part of a strong value proposition for the BoP segment.

Looking at the critical success factor of distribution, no recognizable pattern can be identified among the experts. The only commonality is the reliance on local third-party distributors to cut costs and to ensure the availability of medicine. The main advantage of this approach is the better possibilities of local distributors to reach areas that are difficult to access. But often these distributors exploit the dependency of the pharmaceutical companies and the patients by adding high mark-ups to producer prices, hence increasing the end price. Experts mention mark-ups by "middlemen" (distributors, wholesalers, pharmacies) that add significantly to cost, sometimes up to "a level of 800%" (Expert 4). The experts complain that there are no regulations to cap the level of mark-ups. In order to prevent this, one company successfully collaborates with partners in SSA countries that see the business opportunity in a low-cost offer (= potential increase in volume). They enter into a contractual commitment to charge a low consumer price and, simultaneously, the partners guarantee the continuous supply of drugs. For this to be facilitated and to raise the partners' efficiency, one expert mentions the use of apps and technology to monitor stocks, increase supply performance, and to raise cost-effectiveness.

All experts agree that production has to be as cost-effective as possible to ensure affordability. As discussed in the previous section, companies pursue different approaches depending on their internal situation and their strategy. All the approaches to offer products at low cost mentioned are second to the idea of economies of scale. Based on the value proposition of affordability for the large BoP market segment the aim is to generate large volumes that allow for the use of economies of scale:

> If I reduce the price, I need volumes to go up to balance the lower price. (Expert 4)

Local production is not mentioned as an option by the experts, and interviewees express that this is often more expensive and leaves no room to cut costs.

The critical levers for the volume approach are an affordable price and guaranteed availability of products to the BoP. Only then is the use of economies of scale, and the resulting low per-unit costs, feasible:

> Something that was unaffordable can be made affordable (and profitable) because you have a lower cost of goods. (Expert 1)

The described variety of approaches to ensure efficient value generation in order to comply with the affordability criterion indicates that there is not one single patent remedy. The optimum solution depends on local conditions and the multinational pharmaceutical company's situation. There is still scope to conceptualize and experiment with efficient value generation schemes when addressing the BoP market especially when it comes to distribution (value delivery).

6.2.4 Value Capture and Revenue Model

Value capture today and in the future in a population segment that does not yet provide a functioning market requires measures to create awareness of the offering. When it comes to the BoP market for pharmaceuticals this is not yet well developed. "[...] health awareness in Africa is significantly lower" (Expert 3). The experts agree on the importance of creating visibility and awareness with patients and with governments in order to develop the BoP market and to address it efficiently. Hence, not only the right products but also health education and health-related knowledge is needed, since BoP consumers are often not well educated and have limited access to information. This can lead to the wrong use of medicines and lower treatment success which, in turn, can lead to mistrust of new medication amongst BoP consumers. As a consequence, it might also result in reduced funding by NGOs and governments. This is why companies offer healthcare education that is provided by local private partners, NGOs, and government institutions. Educational and awareness measures named by the experts primarily include the training of healthcare professionals. The majority of experts state that they specifically target training doctors and nurses on the correct use of medicine by organizing symposiums and running education and training programs for medical staff. The second set of awareness-creating measures is health education for patients. Almost all interviewed companies offer services to deliver health education to patients. In one case the multinational firm employs 100 "educators" going from village to village to talk about health-related topics. The activities of the educators include health education meetings on hygiene and nutrition, common prevalent conditions, and self-management of disease in order to increase awareness of diseases, information on prevention, and the importance of health in general. One localized service that some companies offer is the provision of time and a place for local screening, diagnosis, and consultation of patients. Here doctors can prescribe medication and perform treatment if necessary.

All experts mention that there is a clear distinction between the social/philanthropic and the business side. The purpose of awareness measures is not to promote companies' products but to improve the difficult healthcare situation. Nevertheless, in general, this is of strategic importance as creating health awareness is an integral part of creating demand and developing the market for pharmaceuticals at the BoP. This will expand the customer base in the long run and generate volumes large enough for economies of scale to kick in.

The revenue model describes how a business model is financially viable and includes aspects such as cost structure and revenue generation. A consensus among experts exists on how the medicine is sold, which is no different to the conventional way in other markets. Salespeople approach clinics, doctors, pharmacies, or government institutions and try to convince them of the benefits of their products ("pull creation"). However, the cultural diversity and linguistic heterogeneity across regions requires cultural sensitivity and local players. Another common approach in some SSA countries is to participate in public tenders. Tenders are large volume and usually distribution is performed by government institutions. However, some experts share the opinion that public tendering entails difficulties. Firstly, governments often try to push prices to an unsustainably low level where even the cost of goods sold cannot be recovered. Secondly, public healthcare systems, if available, frequently provide inadequate healthcare for patients and are often unaffordable to BoP consumers. A different revenue model is followed by one of the multinational pharmaceutical companies. It generates revenue from royalty fees of the licensed business to an Indian generics drug manufacturer. Other companies mention the development of a second brand or branded generics where the cost of development and approval are significantly lower.

6.2.5 Collaboration

In order to ensure availability and create awareness but also, in some instances, ensure affordability, all multinational pharmaceutical companies interviewed cooperate with local partners in order to address the BoP. These partners are local distributors, faith-based organizations, NGOs, ministries, and other government institutions. With the exception of most local private distributors, these other partners can process large quantities, which is in line with the economies of scale approach of BoP business models on the value generation side. What is mostly lacking is including the BoP population in the business model, as BoP 2.0 proponents in the literature suggest.

Collaboration partners are mainly found in the context of distribution channels and are hence critical for the availability of and access to medicine of BoP customers. The experts mention several types of *intermediaries* with whom they collaborate: distributors of every size, wholesalers, and pharmacies. Experts agree that, especially for BoP business, middlemen are critical partners to reach their customers, in particular in the rural communities. Local partners can provide access to consumers using their established infrastructure. However, one expert emphasizes that the role and importance of the middlemen strongly depends on the region and whether they have an existing and functioning distribution infrastructure. In some countries, one of the companies interviewed has an agreement with its distributor to ensure the availability of a specific amount of medicine to BoP project partner clinics. In other countries, the firm did not find reliable partners that could guarantee this service. This shows that one practical challenge in addressing the BoP along the lines of BoP 2.0 proponents is to find qualified partners in the BoP (and locally in general). Experts widely agree that the distribution of medicine can look different in every country but usually includes a partner. The majority of experts agree that a mission fit with the middlemen is an essential success factor for a BoP business model to achieve affordability. According to one expert, this fit ideally goes all the way to the small pharmacists at the end of the value chain. Only if all partners have the mission to create affordable access to medicine to the BoP and if they have a trust-relationship can the business model be successful. This is also crucial to avoid the high mark-ups that some distributors (and retailers) add to the producer price, raising the end price beyond the affordability level of BoP consumers.

A second group of important collaborators is *government and public institutions*. During the interviews, the experts mentioned that the government and public institutions are always involved in some way. The government plays various roles and exerts different influences in the local pharmaceutical market. The most apparent role is that of the regulator, who is responsible for drug approval and import regulations, among other things. Experts see this role as being inadequately fulfilled. Second, the government is responsible for the healthcare system and can prioritize health interventions and activities. This impacts the type of business that multinational drug companies can engage in with the BoP. Third, the government and its related institutions are major buyers of pharmaceutical products, usually via tender business. Lastly, the government can act as a distributor: multinational pharmaceutical companies sell their medication to the government at a low price in substantial quantities, and distribution is then managed through public healthcare institutions. Hence, the government contributes to the value delivery of the companies' business models.

Public institutions can also be crucial partners for carrying out health awareness projects. The extent to which public institutions are involved depends not only on the country's government but often also on the regional and community institutions in a country. One expert claims that governments often have a negative attitude toward multinational pharmaceutical companies accusing them of "milking" their country and only looking for a profit. Against this backdrop it is difficult to win a tender. In contrast, another expert describes a good reputation and strong government ties. This is the result of many years of operation in the countries which have created employment through major long-term investments by building clinics and hospitals. He goes on to highlight the role of good relations with the government and an on-site presence (localization, see below) for business at the BoP:

> Governments are also looking at other things that a company is doing in the country; they want to see some investment. That makes it easier to win a tender, and this is crucial. If you do not get the tender it is all for nothing. (Expert 2)

Other experts agree on the importance of strong governmental ties and collaboration in order to push for public projects that increase the accessibility of the BoP population to medicines in the countries. Experts mention that they try to push for system change to achieve reimbursement for their products from insurers. Currently, even countries with a healthcare insurance system usually do not refund private spending on drugs but only for health services. In addition, existing healthcare systems are said to be inefficient, often corrupt, and unsustainable.

The third group of typical collaborators are *non-governmental organizations (NGOs)*. They can take on different roles within a business model: First and foremost, they function as a distributor because they may have own distribution centers and clinics. Second, NGOs are customers, who buy large volumes. However, one expert raises the concern that relying on NGOs as customers is often not sustainable. They depend on donations that are continuously decreasing, they often make one-off bulk-purchases which are no solution for non-communicable diseases, and NGOs sometimes negotiate low prices that are not necessarily passed on to patients. Experts state that the nature and quality of the cooperation with NGOs differ across countries depending on the ecosystem of the particular market and the local structures in place. All interviewed managers agree that the use of existing infrastructure as a platform is the main advantage and success factor related to their collaboration with NGOs. Some experts mention good experiences with faith-based organizations that run private hospitals and therefore act as collaborative partners and customers. They organize health-related events for education, perform diagnostic and treatment services, or purchase medicine for their own hospitals and specialized clinics. Other experts consider NGOs in general, faith-based in particular, as partners in corporate social responsibility (CSR) and philanthropic activities. These projects are not directly linked to the business but they nonetheless help to create awareness and acceptability among the BoP population.

6.2.6 *Inclusiveness and Localization*

Experts mention the important role of local governments and authorities but also of primary health workers at the national and provincial levels. Trusting local partners is important to ensure availability (stock-keeping) and in order for the planned price strategy of the multinational pharmaceutical companies targeting the BoP segment to work (affordability).

> Unless you understand how these [local] communities work and select the right partners it will be practically impossible to start a business or get anything done. [...] Local connections are key everywhere in the world to understand local markets. But in Africa they are even more important for navigating the regulations, winning approvals, and gaining access to resources like land and finances. (Mudida and Lago 2015)

Local companies—usually not from the BoP segment itself—work as distributors on the spot. One company has localized the last-mile distribution to the local BoP communities. The aim is to bring the medicine to the BoP population for whom traveling costs to the next pharmacy or other outlet is prohibitive (accessability). Here the idea is to reduce the cost by involving the local BoP population and, at the same time, increase availability. Such an approach is also mentioned in the literature. It has been proposed to run a more community-based delivery system in SSA which will increase accessibility to medication and health services (Zekeng 2016). This is in line with a BoP 2.0 logic as presented in Sect. 2.3. One expert mentions a local company working as a formulator of capsules, pills, and the like for the multinational drug company that addresses the BoP. Sometimes the medication is imported in bulk and locally (re-)packaged. As consumption in the BoP is cash-flow driven, packaging sizes need to be smaller. Thus, localization and its beneficial effects need to be communicated to customers and are an important success factor. Two of the companies interviewed attempt to include people from the local communities in their business approach. However, they find that cultural differences are a barrier to efficient cooperation, a factor that needs to be dealt with. Overall, the interviews showed little evidence of localization activities and approaches to include BoP communities into the business model for the BoP market. Currently the business approach of the interviewed multinational pharmaceutical companies is structured mostly along the lines of BoP 1.0 (see Chap. 2).

6.3 Discussion, Recommendations, and Limitations of Empirical Results

From the interviews conducted with multinational pharmaceutical companies involved in BoP business, some recommendations have emerged. They can be clustered into three aspects: Competence-building, customization, and long-term commitment.

1. Competence-building is about acquiring the skill-set and knowledge necessary to operate at the BoP. According to the majority of the experts, deep knowledge of the market is crucial, as it is in any other market. However, the BoP market is very different to the conventional markets usually addressed by the multinational pharmaceutical companies. The recommendation is to carefully analyze health and business-related matters, to assess the market potential, and to identify any factors needed in the BoP business model. The data has to be ranked, rated, and prioritized in order to identify suitable markets. Participating countries need to be carefully selected implying that the BoP business might not be feasible in every country. In addition, deep and detailed knowledge and understanding of the BoP-specific environment and, even more importantly, of the BoP consumers and their needs is a pre-requisite to draw up a strong value proposition and create a relevant value generation system. As international pharmaceutical firms do not usually work in BoP markets their knowledge of customers and structures is limited. This is one key reason for the importance of localization and local cooperation in BoP business models.
2. Customization is about adjusting business approaches to local conditions. Depending on the country, the elements of the business model need to be designed differently in order to meet the local requirements of the BoP segment and business environment. This means using (or dealing with) existing infrastructure challenges in the most efficient way. Differences in business conditions require adaptation to local requirements of the offered portfolio, choice of partner, and the amount of investment across all business model elements. What is not clear is how substantial and widespread this adjustment needs to be. BoP customers' behavior and circumstances as much as general business conditions are likely to display many similarities across most emerging markets, also going beyond SSA. This would allow for the presumption that certain BoP business model prototypes can be identified so that the extent of customization to local needs is limited, meaning, in turn, that merely *adapting* an existing business model will be sufficient in most cases. Some level of business model scalability seems to be possible across Emerging Markets. Agreement on the need for customization or adaption of value delivery activities exists while less needs to be done in terms of value creation. Thus, making use of economies of scale—where appropriate—is still possible.
3. A long-term commitment is necessary to see profit and success. Multinational pharmaceutical companies have to be aware that successful business at the BoP

requires investment (e.g., construction of clinics) and potentially extended periods of time until break-even is reached. This comes with a certain risk and uncertainty because the approach might not have been tested before. This condition can create internal conflicts and requires much convincing, alignment, and effort. A long-term commitment should go hand in hand with localization to add to the knowledge about the BoP market and consumers (see competence-building). This improves the position to involve the BoP population into the business model's value generating, especially the value delivery, aspects (inclusiveness).

These recommendations are relevant for all companies that want to target the BoP in SSA. They provide an indication of the direction and give information about necessary actions to address the market.

Throughout the interviews, it became clear that the design of business models for the BoP strongly relates to the importance that the companies attach to this market. It varies significantly from high strategic importance to relatively low importance. All experts agree that revenue from the BoP business is significantly lower and not comparable to other markets. On the one hand, the higher the importance attached to BoP markets the more attention is paid to a sustainable business model with a long-term focus that requires innovation and resources. It requires pharmaceutical companies to come up with new solutions and to think about details since it is a true innovation task. Furthermore, managers have to learn from scratch how to set up the revenue model and how to organize their value generation activities. Surprisingly, the strategy is to find solutions that can be executed globally (scalability) with local adaptations. On the other hand, when BoP business is of secondary importance to the company's management, the business tends to be outsourced or licensed and a regular fee is the income driver. There are some multinational drug firms that attach a "medium" importance to the BoP. They use various measures that increase the availability and affordability of medicine for the BoP without sacrificing quality. For these companies, there is no underlying strategic or structured business approach but business at the BoP is considered to be potentially interesting for the future. Therefore, they engage in business activities with the BoP as far as possible without making major adjustments to their existing business models.

On the one hand, differences in the approach of multinational pharmaceutical companies can be seen in each of the business model elements. On the other hand, some similarities exist. In general, the experts say little with regard to the BoP segment that goes beyond the role of customers and target group. If localization is done it is on a national level and little emphasis is placed on the BoP market itself. There is also agreement on the critical role of collaboration with local partners. The key partners are local distributors, governments, and NGOs. Here the focus lies especially on the distribution channel for the last mile. Hence, the idea of tapping into the potential of the BoP population, which underlies the logic of BoP 2.0 (see Sect. 2.3), is not (yet) realized. Multinational pharmaceutical companies still treat the BoP markets in SSA mainly along the lines of BoP 1.0, where the role of the BoP population is limited to that of customers. The question arises whether innovative approaches exist on how to involve the BoP population more along the value chain, in the sense of inclusiveness. The side effect will be to generate income and thus raise the purchasing power as argued by Prahalad (2006). Cultural differences undoubtedly exist but there are fewer cultural differences between potential partners at the BoP and the BoP consumers which could be exploited if inclusiveness were strengthened. The interviews showed that companies are not yet thinking about innovative ways to specifically access the BoP segment. Their models are still much based on conventional approaches such as tender and NGO-business.

All business models are based on economies of scale to achieve affordability. How this is achieved varies from company to company and country to country. All companies are involved in different types of awareness creation to increase demand and, hence, volumes. One point that all experts, bar one, failed to mention is the perspective of economies of scale on a global level:

> [...] when you think about business models, don't think about them with a clear regional focus but rather with a global view. Then, try to find out how you can adapt them to target the local needs actually but secure the ability to scale up at a certain level as much as possible. (Expert 5)

Therefore, the underlying idea of addressing the BoP is about selling extra volumes which allows for economies of scale reducing the per-unit cost in the (global) factory. This allows for higher profit margins in markets with higher end-consumer price levels while, at the same time, contributing to the success factor of affordability (on the level of producer prices) for the BoP markets. Lower prices—if they reach the BoP consumers—lead to higher sales volumes. In addition, the extra (global) profits can be used to generate additional volume in BoP markets by means of market development activities (cross-subsidization). Whether or not this materializes depends on the capacity utilization of the global factories of the multinational pharmaceutical companies. However, it can be an important lever for the global profitability levels of the companies.

The result of economies of scale is low producer prices which—in many cases—does not have the desired impact on consumer prices and on affordability. The consumer price is critically dependent on low distribution and overhead costs. If distribution costs are high the achieved low production costs will not be transferred to the ultimate price payable by the BoP consumers. This in turn will not lead to the required volume effect that is needed for the BoP business model to be sustainable. The experts mention their difficulty to access BoP customers, especially in rural areas. This implies that logistical distribution costs are significant. Experts point out that high distribution costs threaten access to the BoP market, which potentially disturbs the high-volume, low-price approach of the multinational pharmaceutical companies. These additional distribution costs are hard to control for the pharmaceutical companies.

So far it seems that there is insufficient involvement of the BoP population in the BoP business model of pharmaceutical companies. Especially from the perspective of packaging (value creation) and the distribution of the "last mile" (value delivery), there seems to be some potential to lower mark-ups on the producer price making drugs more affordable. Success at the BoP is only realistic if multinational pharmaceutical companies have a strategic focus and commitment to address the BoP markets in SSA. It also needs innovative approaches to address these challenges when doing business on the BoP markets.

Despite the contribution of this empirical analysis to the research gap and the practical value of the analysis, some limitations exist. The number of expert interviews and, hence, the generated data was limited. Despite the fact that, in general, only a few pharmaceutical MNCs exist and, of those, only a small sample is active in addressing the BoP in SSA it would be beneficial to include additional cases and more experts in future studies. Nonetheless, the case population is small so that the selected sample is representative of ongoing activities. The limited number of cases investigated stresses the explorative and inductive character of this study.

The method of collecting data through semi-structured interviews provides a good overview of relevant company topics with respect to their BoP business. But a strictly explorative approach might have yielded new and more out-of-the-box results. In addition, the time limits of the interviews may have curtailed more in-depth answers, which might have added to a deeper understanding of the business model elements in practice. However, to remain on a level where data can be compared and summarized, the information has to be at a certain (high) level. The purpose of this book's investigation was rather broad, trying to understand the entire business model at the BoP. This results in a holistic, systematic understanding of business models at the BoP as opposed to a detailed analysis of individual aspects of a business model. Hence, future research should focus on specific aspects of BoP business models and dive more deeply into the topic for a more thorough analysis. This implies a different selection of experts to be interviewed, thus, adding perspectives.

References

Anderson J (2006) A structured approach for bringing mobile telecommunications to the world's poor. Electron J Inf Syst Dev Countries 27:1–9

Atteslander P (2000) Methoden der empirischen Sozialforschung. Walter de Gruyter, Berlin

Cropley AJ (2002) Qualitative Forschungsmethoden: Eine praxisnahe Einführung. Verlag Dietmar Klotz, Eschborn

Garz D, Kraimer K (1991) Qualitativ-empirische Sozialforschung: Konzepte, Methoden, Analysen. Westdeutscher Verlag, Opladen

Gläser J, Laudel G (2006) Experteninterviews und qualitative Inhaltsanalyse. 2., durchgesehene Auflage. Springer VS, Wiesbaden

Graneheim UH, Lundman B (2004) Qualitative content analysis in nursing research: concepts, procedures and measures to achieve trustworthiness. Nurse Educ Today 24:105–112

Gummesson E, Nenonen S, Storbacka K (2010) Business model design: conceptualizing networked value co-creation. Int J Qual Serv Sci 2:43–59

Hogerzeil H, Helt SF, Hill S, Kamoga R, Laing R, Nguyen A, Pisani E, Ross-Degnan D, Shah D, Viñes Fiestas H (2016) Access to Medicine Index 2016. Access to Medicine Foundation, Haarlem

Kromrey H (1998) Empirische Sozialforschung: Modelle und Methoden der Datenerhebung und Datenauswertung. Springer VS, Wiesbaden

Kuckartz U (2010) Einführung in die computergestützte Analyse qualitativer Daten, 3., aktualisierte Aufl. Springer VS, Wiesbaden

Mayring P (2010) Qualitative Inhaltsanalyse: Grundlagen und Techniken, 11., aktualisierte und überarb. Aufl. Beltz, Weinheim

Mayring P, Gläser-Zikuda M (2008) Die Praxis der Qualitativen Inhaltsanalyse. Weinheim, Beltz

Mudida R, Lago A (2015) A roadmap to opportunities – five pillars for doing business in Africa. IESE Insight 24:15–23

Prahalad CK (2006) The fortune at the bottom of the pyramid: eradicating poverty through profits. Wharton School Publishing, Upper Saddle River, NJ

Saunders M, Lewis P, Thornhill A (2012) Research methods for business students, 5th edn. Pearson Education Limited, Harlow

Zekeng E (2016) Healthcare systems in Sub-Saharan Africa: focusing on community-based delivery (CBD) of health services and the development of local research institutes. United Nations Peace Progr 3:44–49

Chapter 7
Conclusion, Conceptual Framework, and Future Research

In the previous chapters, the insights of the literature on business models for the BoP markets and the results of the empirical analysis on multinational pharmaceutical companies in SSA were presented. In order to move the inquiry forward, the results of the literature and empirical analysis are contrasted and scrutinized with regard to the research question. Finally, a conceptual business model recommendation will be provided.

7.1 Conclusion

The literature review of the BoP concept and business models draws a multi-faceted picture for both topics and identifies various research gaps. There have been limited attempts to combine both research areas—on business models and on the BoP—to guide practical business activities at the BoP in SSA. It is likely that the shortage of analysis is a result of the research areas being relatively recent, with little consensus among researchers. One example is the blurred definition of the BoP population as a target group for which various descriptions about the income level of the BoP population exist. This different understanding is reflected in the outcome of this study, where multinational pharmaceutical companies highlight that they do not regard the entire BoP as a target group for their business model. A clear income level from which a business approach starts to make business sense cannot be identified clearly, but a lower limit of an annual income of around USD1000 PPP seems reasonable. However, multinational pharmaceutical companies need to have a clear understanding of the characteristics and income patterns of the BoP consumers as a target group. Researchers (Rangan et al. 2007) and practitioners alike propose a segmentation within the BoP emphasizing that people in extreme poverty have to be addressed with philanthropy. The relevant BoP market size in SSA is significant, as Sect. 4.4 showed.

P. von Carlowitz, *Success in the Bottom of the Pyramid Market in Africa*, SpringerBriefs in Business, https://doi.org/10.1007/978-3-030-59068-0_7

Scholars and practitioners require more in-depth research on business models for BoP markets (Schuster and Holtbrügge 2014). There is still too much of a "one size fits all" expectation among private sector companies (Kubzansky 2012). Some authors even criticize research on business models operating at the BoP as theoretically and conceptually ambiguous (Seelos 2010). Nakata (2012) agrees and states that the BoP literature offers little practical and theoretical knowledge to guide firms that try to address their products and services to the needs of BoP consumers. Only a few scholars have studied organizational structures, functional routines, and management practices that enable the private sector to establish business activities in BoP markets (Ramachandran et al. 2012). Tashman and Marano (2010) point out that a need exists to theoretically and empirically analyze beneficial strategies that have been obtained from case studies. In this context, Kolk et al. (2014) stress that business failures seem to be ignored and disregarded. The authors see the necessity to investigate real failures in all their aspects to understand what went wrong, where, and why. The empirical analysis in Chap. 6 confirms this lack of focus on BoP-specific needs and the business environment and in consequence a limited "customization" of business approaches to the BoP. If at all, the companies interviewed adjust minor aspects of their general business model when trying to enter the BoP markets. Adjustments mentioned by experts mostly relate to the success factor of affordability.

With a view to the business model elements analyzed, a consensus between theory and practice exists regarding the value proposition. According to literature and practitioners, affordability, awareness, access, and availability are necessary attributes for an attractive offering in the BoP context. Reducing the quality of drugs is not an option from either perspective. While creating awareness is only one of the principles mentioned by the literature, empirical analysis reveals that this aspect is very important for the pharmaceutical industry. This can be explained by the need to develop the medicine market aimed at the BoP population. Divergent views are found about the significance of innovative products for the BoP market. Researchers address the need for innovative goods and services (Karamchandani et al. 2011) whereas practitioners mention the option of using existing and older products that are low-cost.

Arguably the most relevant success factor at the BoP is affordability. A volume-based business model that is driven by achieving scale in order to make a profit is a fundamental aspect when it comes to lowering the producer price. Increasing access and awareness of potential customers is a key driver of volume. When it comes to customer price—the real measure of affordability—the empirical study points to a practical challenge: Private distributors frequently add very high mark-ups onto the producer price and thus raise the consumer price substantially. This is not described in detail in the literature. If affordability is to be achieved, the high distribution costs need to be addressed, which means the value generation element, especially value delivery, needs to be adjusted. With regard to distribution costs, literature and experts agree that strong partnerships and collaboration are required for a successful business at the BoP. However, practitioners leave the issue more or less unresolved while the BoP literature (BoP 2.0) provides three strategies that should shape value generation for successful business at the BoP. These are (1) integrating the BoP population into the value chain (inclusion); (2) cooperating with NGOs (collaboration); and (3) building local capacity (localization) in order to improve the conditions in BoP markets. While analyzing the data this can partly be confirmed for the pharmaceutical industry, especially the collaboration aspect. Inclusion and localization are yet to be systematically integrated into companies' BoP business models. The literature sees a value-added role of BoP communities mainly in the value delivery part (Zekeng 2016) but also low-skilled tasks on the value creation side (for instance re-packaging). However, activities on the value creation side mostly imply some type of investment in a facility, which can act as a deterrent to companies.

Regarding the value generation issue, the literature provides little insight into how exactly value can be generated for the BoP successfully. The empirical investigation does not provide a unique solution or pattern because many internal and external factors influence value generation activities. Internal factors are the difference in the strategic importance of BoP initiatives, whether multinational pharmaceutical companies can rely on experiences in the countries or the product portfolio. External factors are differences in countries, regions, stakeholder influence, and disease burden. In contrast to the literature, the statements of the experts make it clear that multinational pharmaceutical companies have to approach every country or region differently. At the same time, some experts mention the importance of scalability. Concurrent customization and scalability creates a BoP dilemma.

In conclusion, the interviews indicate that there is not one correct approach for multinational pharmaceutical companies. Instead, a strategic choice of measures has to be made individually according to the characteristics of the respective multinational pharmaceutical company. However, all companies interviewed are pursuing a volume-based business model as a prototype. The differences are with regard to HOW they achieve the required volume for the use of economies of scale. A framework consolidating all the findings and showing the inter-dependency between the business model elements and considering the success factors discussed provides a conceptional answer to the research question of this book:

> How do business models of multinational pharmaceutical companies have to be designed to profitably access the Bottom of the Pyramid market in Sub-Saharan Africa?

The findings of this research based on literature and empirical analysis lead to some conceptual insights on the functioning of business models for the BoP in SSA.

7.2 Conceptual Framework

Based on the assessment of the empirical findings and the literature review, Fig. 7.1 presents a business model concept that explains the structure of a promising business model for the BoP market. It tries to consolidate both literature and empirical findings.

Value Generation - Creation	Value Proposition	Value Generation - Delivery	Customer Segment
• Economies of scale production • Outsourcing • Selection of portfolio offered to BoP based on – Cost considerations – Generics – Drugs for high disease burden treatment	• Affordability • Quality • Availability	• Awareness creation for market development purposes • Availability through distribution • Collaboration in availability and awareness with – Distributors – Public institutions – NGOs	Bottom of the Pyramid • Low income • Out-of-pocket spending on drugs • Price sensitive • Hard to reach

Cost	Revenue Model – Value Capture
• Cost of goods sold (COGS) • Distribution cost (to partner) • Cost for awareness and market development activities	• Tender business • Distributor business • License fee

Fig. 7.1 BoP business model prototype based on empirical analysis. Source: Own illustration based on business model canvas logic

The analyzed elements of a business model for the BoP—that is value proposition, value generation, revenue model—are inter-related as should be the case in a strong business model. Looking at the value proposition, the findings of the analysis indicate that drugs and health services offered should meet the criteria of affordability, availability, and quality. These are all relevant factors given the needs and requirements of BoP customers who are, in general, price-sensitive due to their poverty (affordability) and are also difficult to reach (availability). The revenue model should contain an income engine that enables long-term stability with the value-generating activities making it happen. These two elements—revenue model and value generation—ensure that value is delivered to the BoP customer and that value is captured by the multinational pharmaceutical company. The mechanics of the volume-based business model using economies of scale at the center of the revenue model to achieve the affordable selling prices is presented in Fig. 7.2.

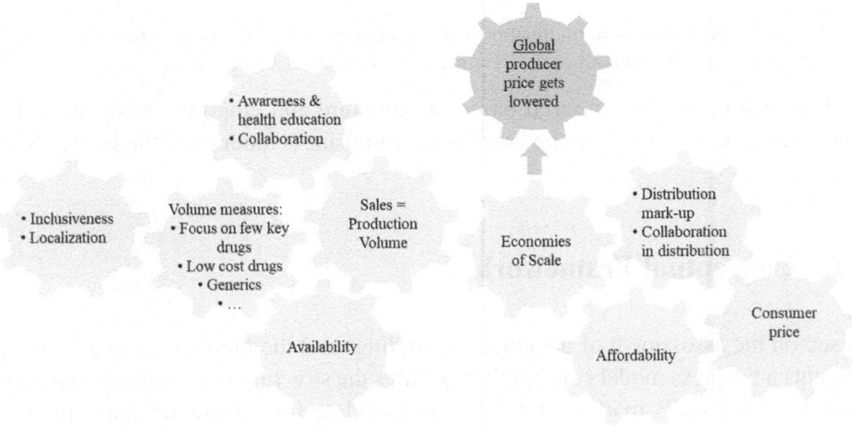

Fig. 7.2 Literature and empirical results: mechanics of a BoP business model. Source: Own illustration

Most multinational pharmaceutical companies follow the mechanics of the BoP business model prototype as described: For the value proposition to be delivered, the value-generating activities focus on economies of scale. The mechanics of the BoP volume-based business model emphasize the role of generating volume in production and thus lowering the per-unit-cost, hence, the producer price. This lower per-unit production cost can also be leveraged in global high-price markets and thus increase profits there. This is feasible depending on the capacity utilization level of global factories and whether they manufacture the same medicines needed in the BoP market.

Volume generation is supported along the value chain by various measures of awareness creation to develop the market and create demand. Volume raising measures include activities to ensure availability, focus on a few medicines aimed at the main disease burden at the BoP, and a limited offering of standard and low-cost generic medication. The resulting volume results in economies of scale. However, the critical point for keeping the value proposition's promise of affordable prices to BoP consumers depends on the distribution cost, that is on value delivery.

When it comes to distribution, multinational pharmaceutical companies typically collaborate with governments, NGOs, and/or private distributors. Therefore, the distribution costs are out of their control. Governments and NGOs are usually one-off large tenders but are no basis for building a continuous business, particularly since governments often struggle to finance tenders. This is why private local distributors play an important role if companies want to set up a systematic and long-term business. The challenge mentioned by experts is the high mark-ups on producer prices sometimes raising consumer prices beyond affordability. Thus, the large gap between producer price and consumer price paid by the BoP customers is a potential threat to the business model's success. This is why the most critical point of the BoP business model is not the value creation side but rather the value delivery part of value generation. In practice and in the literature some ideas to deal with this challenge have been mentioned. A contractual agreement with a reliable distributor that includes guarantees on a continuous supply of drugs (availability) and limits the size of mark-ups (affordability) is one way to approach the costs of value delivery. The reliability of such an arrangement is based on either self-commitment and contractual agreement—as described by one expert. Only when distributors agree to the volume and mark-up conditions are they eligible to cooperate with the multinational pharmaceutical companies. For this to work, such a local distributor needs to be available. The use of technology can help to increase availability as it helps local partners to monitor their stock and make distribution more cost-efficient. In addition, micro-credit models for small pharmacies can enable them to hold more stock. If the volume distributed to the BoP is high, it will still be an attractive business for the distributor.

Another, hitherto underdeveloped, approach to reducing distribution costs is based on localizing more of the value-generating business aspects and focusing on more inclusion of the BoP population. Localization and inclusion have been propagated in the literature, in the concepts of BoP 2.0 and BoP 3.0, as important when addressing the BoP market. So far they have not featured widely in the companies' approaches. Inclusiveness is possible on both the value creation side which is, however, limited by the low skill level and, more realistically, the value delivery side in terms of (last mile) distribution. Localization and involving the BoP population may be one way to control the level of mark-ups and create a partnership of equals. This has three advantages: (1) They are low-cost, (2) they are motivated and identify with the mission, and (3) they know the conditions and characteristics of BoP consumers. Most of them are not trained for medical tasks but can be deployed for simple tasks such as teaching basic hygienic behavior and performing the physical "last mile" distribution. For this to be possible, a greater level of localization is needed in order to coordinate these efforts. This can go as far as the expansion of healthcare facilities, be they clinics or "health camps" that offer consultation and medication close to the BoP customers. With this availability demand for drugs is generated via the creation of awareness. It can be financed with the help of public–private partnerships. A level of insourcing of activities previously done by the distributors is required. Thus, companies would and should move more toward a BoP 2.0 approach and involve the BoP population in the value generation activities of the business model. What this discussion implies—and here literature and practitioners agree—is a long-term commitment to the BoP market by the companies' top management.

What has been presented here is a business model prototype for BoP business whose basic mechanics work for all companies in many countries. How volume is generated and how availability is generated using efficient distribution varies from company to company depending on their internal conditions and on the general and BoP-specific market conditions in each country. This is where some level of customization or adaptation is needed. Some of the different measures used were shown in the empirical analysis and discussed in Chap. 6. However, the basic approach of the business model is scalable and requires adjustment mainly on the value delivery side.

7.3 Contribution and Future Research

Although a lot more research on the BoP is required, this book contributes by filling research gaps that have been identified (see Chap. 3). To begin with, this work extends the level of knowledge about the BoP business in SSA and complements the work that has been done on Asia's BoP markets. A combination of the BoP concept and business model design is rarely observed in theoretical or empirical studies, especially in the SSA context. This book develops a conceptual framework for business models of multinational pharmaceutical companies targeting the BoP in SSA. The present study combines a literature review with empirical findings from semi-structured expert interviews. It thus combines the academic with the practical perspective to understand and develop a feasible business model concept for the BoP market, thus providing practical relevance. It also contributes to the limited empirical literature on business models for BoP markets in general and especially with a focus on SSA. Furthermore, the expert interviews provide insights into individual challenges to design a successful business model and into the strategic importance of BoP initiatives in companies that have not been found in academic literature to date.

Based on these contributions and analysis, some areas for future research have been identified. Although this book provides an empirical analysis of business models for BoP markets, it has focused on the overall business model and its mechanics. What it does not explicitly provide is an in-depth empirical analysis of specific success factors and possibilities to overcome challenges when addressing the BoP as a multinational company. Two aspects in particular need further consideration and investigation as they are main obstacles and open issues for successful business models at the BoP in SSA: (1) Value delivery and (2) Possibilities of inclusiveness and localization. The first topic refers to the issue of mark-ups and high distribution costs which counter efforts to improve affordability by reducing producer prices through economies of scale. This topic needs further theoretical, and especially empirical, analysis. A practical solution to this issue would be extremely valuable for companies. The second topic is related. For which aspects of value generation (or, for that matter, any other aspect of the business model) is localization worthwhile and for which activities is it more sensible to use an inclusiveness approach. The investigation in this book has indicative evidence that the most potential lies with value delivery (distribution, awareness generation) as it is low-skill, cost-intensive, and local (BoP) knowledge is important. This, however, should be further investigated and understood.

Lastly, the focus in this book was on multinational pharmaceutical companies in SSA. The question of the transferability of the insights to other industries comes to mind. What other types of industry could follow a volume-based business model similar to the one conceived for pharmaceutical companies (and in which countries)? An interesting question not answered in this book is how industries that are not based on economies of scale can set up a profitable and lasting business model for the BoP markets. What will be the mechanics of such a business model?

References

Karamchandani A, Kubzansky M, Lalwani N (2011) Is the bottom of the pyramid really for you. Harv Bus Rev 89:107–111

Kolk A, Rivera-Santos M, Rufín C (2014) Reviewing a decade of research on the "base/bottom of the pyramid" (BOP) concept. Bus Soc 53:338–377

Kubzansky M (2012) The importance of business models. In: Brookings Instituion (ed) Old problems, new solutions: harnessing technology and innovation in the fight against global poverty. The 2012 Brookings Blum Roundtable Policy Beliefs. Brookings Institution, Washington, DC, pp 41–49. https://www.brookings.edu/wp-content/uploads/2016/06/10-blum-roundtable-full-report.pdf. Accessed 3 Mar 2020

Nakata C (2012) From the Special Issue Editor: Creating new products and services for and with the base of the pyramid. J Prod Innov Manag 29:3–5

Ramachandran J, Pant A, Pani SK (2012) Building the BoP producer ecosystem: the evolving engagement of Fabindia with Indian Handloom Artisans. J Prod Innov Manag 29:33–51

Rangan VK, Quelch JA, Herrero G, Barton B (2007) Business solutions for the global poor: creating social and economic value. Wiley, San Francisco

Schuster T, Holtbrügge D (2014) Resource dependency, innovative strategies, and firm performance in BOP markets. J Prod Innov Manag 31:43–59

Seelos C (2010) Theorizing and strategizing with models: generative models of business models. In: IESE business school working paper no. 857. IESE Business School – University of Navarra, Barcelona

Tashman P, Marano V (2010) Dynamic capabilities and base of the pyramid business strategies. J Bus Ethics 89:495–514

Zekeng E (2016) Healthcare systems in Sub-Saharan Africa: focusing on community-based delivery (CBD) of health services and the development of local research institutes. United Nations Peace Progr 3:44–49

The manufacturer's authorised representative in the EU is Springer Nature Customer Service Centre GmbH, Europaplatz 3, 69115 Heidelberg, Germany. If you have any concerns regarding our products, please contact ProductSafety@springernature.com

Printed and bound by CPI Group (UK) Ltd, Croydon, CR0 4YY
30/09/2026
02225467-0012